FINANCIAL FREEDOM

with

REAL ESTATE INVESTING

The Blueprint to Quitting
Your Job with Real Estate –
Even without Experience or Cash

MICHAEL BLANK

Publishing services provided by  **Archangel Ink**

ISBN-13: 978-1-9865-3236-5

ISBN-10: 1986532364

Disclaimer

The information in this book is not meant to replace the advice of a certified professional. Please consult a licensed advisor in matters relating to your livelihood including your mental and physical health, finances, business, family planning, education, and spiritual practices.

If you choose to attempt any of the methods mentioned in this book, the authors and publisher advise you to take full responsibility for your safety and know your limits. The authors and publisher are not liable for any damages or negative consequences from any treatment, action, application, or preparation to any person reading or following the information in this book.

Neither the publisher nor the individual authors shall be liable for any physical, psychological, emotional, financial, or commercial damages, including, but not limited to, special, incidental, consequential, or other damages to the readers of this book.

The content of each chapter is the sole expression and opinion of its author and not necessarily that of the publisher. No warranties or guarantees are expressed or implied by the publisher's choice to include any of the content in this volume.

What Others Are Saying

"Michael has written a must-read book for anyone who wants to quit their job with real estate investing. Read this book, and learn from one of the best ..."

— Ken McElroy, Principal of the MC Companies, Best-Selling Author of "The ABCs of Real Estate Investing", International Speaker and Real Estate Advisor to Robert Kiyosaki

"If You're sick of spending 90% of your day doing things you hate and only 10% doing things you love, then read this book. It shows you how to start your entrepreneurial journey as a real estate investor and create the life you've always dreamed of."

— John Lee Dumas, Founder, EOFire

"If you are looking for a book that will inspire and educate you to pursue financial freedom fast— this book is a must-read. Michael's easy-to-read style and in-depth experience make this book vital for any growing real estate investor."

— Brandon Turner, Host of the BiggerPockets Podcast, Real Estate Investor and Author

"Real estate has created more millionaires than any other investment opportunity. Unlike other investment vehicles, few other than real estate offer the opportunity to invest with other people's money, or to use leverage and magnify your financial performance. Michael gets it, and he's created a blueprint to show you exactly what-to-do! This book is a must read for anyone seeking financial freedom through apartment investing."

— Mike Hambright, FlipNerd.com

"Do you value your time? Good. So does Michael Blank. In his new book, Financial Freedom with Real Estate Investing, he shares practical secrets and tools that will have you ready and ravenous to get started!"

— Joe Fairless, Host of the "Best Real Estate Investing Advice Ever" podcast

"In his debut work, Michael Blank turns the complex world of real estate into a simple to follow process for beginners. Forget get-rich-quick schemes—let Michael show you the key to long-term wealth through multi-family real estate investing."

— Peter Conti, Co-Author, "Commercial Real Estate Investing for Dummies

"It's no secret that real estate investing is a great moneymaker. What few people understand is just how lucrative real estate investing can be. In his breakout work, Financial Freedom with Real Estate Investing, Michael fills that knowledge gap to get you on the path to success, now!"

— Marco Santarelli, Host of the "Passive Real Estate Investing" podcast

"Escaping the 9-5 just became even easier. Pick up Michael Blank's new book and watch your path to financial freedom open before your eyes."

— Keith Weinhold, Owner of Get Rich Education

"Attending Michael's seminar was one of the turning points in my company's success, and this book will pack a powerful punch in helping many along the path to financial freedom."

— Paul Moore, Wellings Capital, Author of "The Perfect Investment"

"Michael is a passionate and purpose-driven entrepreneur that not only teaches but inspires. This is evidence of the massive success that his students and podcast listeners have had in acquiring multifamily apartments and becoming financially free themselves. A true professional, Michael provides so much value in every conversation, interaction, and interview and his book is a valuable resource that any multifamily real estate investor would greatly benefit from."

— M.C. Laubscher, The "Cashflow Ninja"

"Investing in Multi-family units might appear out of reach for the average Joe, but Michael busts that myth wide open. He reveals how anyone can get started with real estate, regardless of background. This blueprint is the kick-start you've been searching for."

— Jake & Gino

"Financial Freedom with Real Estate Investing captures what it takes to generate wealth with real estate: A solid work ethic, battle hardened grit, and the guts to take calculated risks."

— Reed Goossens, Host of the Investing in the US Podcast

Author's Note

As you'll see, this book covers a lot of ground. To help keep this text as concise as possible, many of the how-to details have not been included. However, they are available to you in the form of a free Companion Course. The course includes downloadable templates, bonus video content, and other resources to accelerate your journey to financial freedom with real estate. I reference the appropriate resources throughout this book, so if you don't register now, you can still do so later. But now is always better than later, right?

So make sure you register for the free course now while it's still fresh in your mind.

You can access the free Companion Course at:

FinancialFreedomTheBook.com/course.

Contents

Introduction

Brad Tacia had done everything right: he went to school, got good grades, and then got a good job with benefits working for an established car parts manufacturer in Detroit. He thought he was living the good life.

And then the recession hit his world like a hurricane. Coworkers, friends, and neighbors were being laid off all around him. Would he be next? If he lost his job, how would he provide for his family? Panic seized him. He couldn't sleep at night.

It was a tough time for Brad. But he was lucky—he kept his job through it all. Still, it left a bad taste in his mouth about the "security" of a job. The certainty he'd had about his financial future was shaken to the core, and he and his wife started thinking about a Plan B.

Brad and his wife came up with a plan to buy one rental house per year for ten years, which would then replace their income. They decided to direct the majority of their savings and 401(k) to buy these rentals. In the aftermath of the recession, the rentals in Detroit were cheap but still had good cash flow. Over the next five years, they managed to buy five of these rental houses.

Around this time, things got busy for Brad at work, and he was routinely working more than fifty hours a week and sometimes on call after hours and during weekends. He started to miss his family;

everyone had thought his work schedule was a temporary phase. One night he put his four-year-old daughter to bed, and she asked him if he had to work the next day. As he answered yes, he could see her face drop with disappointment.

That was Brad's breaking point. He needed to accelerate his ten-year retirement plan, and he needed to do it fast or he was going to miss his daughter growing up. So Brad shifted his real estate investing strategy. In the next two years, Brad covered his living expenses using that strategy and was able to quit his job.

Since leaving his job, Brad's been sleeping better, eating better, and he's started exercising. He's able to spend time with his family, and they frequently go on vacation. His relationship with his wife has improved in many ways, and he is getting to know his daughter. Not having to work all day long has opened him up to think more intentionally about his life.

These days, Brad knows he really is living the good life.

It Is Possible to Become Financially Free with Real Estate (but Maybe Not in the Way You Think)

Is Brad's story just a fluke? Did he just get lucky, or is there a strategy at work in Brad's approach that can work for you too? I've been a full-time entrepreneur for over a decade, and in that time, I've interviewed dozens of successful real estate entrepreneurs on my podcast. Based on these years of experience, I am convinced of one thing:

It is possible to become financially free with real estate. The entrepreneurs who achieve financial freedom are like you and me. They want to provide for their families on the one hand, but they also want to control their time. They feel intuitively that there is greatness inside them. But they understand that in order to discover their greatness, they need to address the reality of life, which is to earn a living. They're frustrated by their inability to provide for their families and control their time.

Unlike most real estate investors who attend their local REIA meeting each month, these entrepreneurs have discovered a particular KIND of real estate strategy that has allowed them to quit their jobs in three to five years. This strategy has worked for thousands before them and will work for thousands after them, and they're confident it will also work for them. Most interestingly, they're able to do this without any previous experience and without the cash to pull it off.

Today these men and women have the option to do whatever they want. They control their time. They spend more time with their family. Some travel. Others continue to expand their business to build a legacy. Because their brains are no longer consumed by working all week, these entrepreneurs are able to ponder what else life has to offer. For the first time, they're able to think about a life of purpose and significance.

Financial freedom is a powerful thing that will change your life and your family. I'm going to introduce you to some of these entrepreneurs and show you the exact step-by-step Blueprint to Financial Freedom they used to get there.

Is This Book for You?

If you're interested in achieving financial freedom through real estate, then this book is for you.

You might be looking for a way out of your nine-to-five job. It's okay because it pays the bills, but it doesn't fulfill you. Or maybe you just plain hate your job. Either way, you're looking for a way out. Maybe you're running a small business, but the hours are killing you, and dealing with employees is overwhelming. Maybe you're already investing in single-family houses, but you're burning out and can't see a way to scale the business without losing your sanity. You might be looking for a way to pay for your kids' education or secure your upcoming retirement.

More than that ... you're looking for *passive* income so that you *don't* have to work (unless you want to). So that you can do what you want, where you want, and with whom you want. Whatever your particular situation, you're looking for financial freedom. And you think that real estate is the way to get there.

You would be both right and wrong.

You're right because real estate can, in fact, lead you to financial freedom. But you may be wrong because you're pursuing the wrong strategy—a strategy that is *not* passive, won't scale, or won't help you achieve your financial goals.

You may not initially agree with me. Or even if you do, you might not think you can do it.

That's okay.

It's my job to guide you in a way that will convince you—so that you can believe. By the time you're done reading this book, you will know the exact strategy that will allow you to achieve financial freedom in the next three to five years.

So sit back, relax, learn, and decide to change your life.

Let's start the journey together.

PART I

The Best Real Estate Strategy to Achieving Financial Freedom

CHAPTER 1

My Rocky Road to Financial Freedom

It was January 2015. My restaurants were losing $10,000 a month, and I had nearly maxed out my $200,000 line of credit. I couldn't use the business credit card at Starbucks because it was overdrawn. I was getting nasty letters from the IRS about penalties, interest, and liens.

I had three months left before I would run out of liquidity—that's DEBT liquidity, not CASH! And if that were to happen, I could no longer pay my employees, which meant they would quit and I would have to shut down the store. And if that happened, the landlords would sue me for the remainder of my personally guaranteed lease. Then I would lose my house.

I had bet big on a pizza franchise to achieve the passive income dream, but it turned into a nightmare. And for what? I would have been better off staying with my secure job instead of quitting ten years earlier to follow a dream.

What kind of husband was I?

What kind of father?

What kind of provider?

~

It all started so innocently. My dad made a good living working for IBM his entire career. When we vacationed, we did it right.

Every winter, we would go skiing in Innsbruck, Austria. I'd be in ski school all day for two weeks, and I got pretty good at an early age. We'd go to Hawaii, the Bahamas, or Nova Scotia. Life was pretty good. But I don't remember my dad much because he was working a lot. I remember that when I was in middle school in Germany, I barely saw him.

Like most people, I was taught to get good grades, and getting A's came easy to me. I started off as a biology major in college, but I switched to computer science my sophomore year, because it wasn't clear to me how I was going to make money. When I graduated in 1992, the job market was awful, so I decided to get my masters—also in computer science—at the College of William and Mary.

Getting a secure job that paid well was the logical next step. It was what my parents told me to do and what everybody else was doing. It would also allow me to continue seeing my girlfriend, who I had met a couple of years earlier.

I didn't question it, and I continued to drift through life, doing whatever thing came my way. I became a computer programmer for a government contractor in Northern Virginia and then took a job with the new America Online web development team. It was 1995, and the Internet boom had begun. While AOL was pretty cool, it wasn't nearly as exciting as what was going on in Silicon Valley.

And I wanted a piece of it.

During one of our happy hours, I was chatting with our head of marketing. She told me her husband was starting a software startup not far from the office.

I joined in January of 1997 as their first programmer.

I was in the right place at the right time, and in 2001, the company went public and put a bunch of money in my pocket.

Life was pretty good—at first.

Four years later, I sat in my cubicle not getting much done. I had been at the same company for the past eight years. When I joined, it was an exciting startup, but by five years in, most of the FUN people had left. I hadn't. Now it just felt like a job, and I loathed the office politics.

I also had a young daughter and son, and hated not being there for them during the day. I remember my daughter had a ballet recital, and she asked me if I would watch her. I told her that I was sorry, but I had a work function that evening. I remember the way her face dropped in disappointment.

I used to come home exhausted, with barely enough energy to help with dinner and the kids' bedtime. I'd crash in front of the TV to decompress and then go to bed. On weekends, I ran errands and tried to recharge the batteries so I could do it all over again on Monday.

I felt like the years were passing me by, and I was missing my kids grow up. I was making good money, but I wasn't able to spend time with my family. What I really wanted was control over my time. But I had to work to provide for my family. I couldn't figure out how to get both.

Then in 2004, when I was thirty-three years old, I read the book *Rich*

Dad Poor Dad, and it hit me like a ton of bricks. I thought, *I'm such an idiot. It's not how much you earn or have in the bank account—it's about how much passive income you have.*

I read the book in about a day, and it completely changed my entire financial outlook. Passive income was going to change my life. It would allow me to be financially free so that I didn't have to work, and I could do whatever I wanted to do. It would allow me to provide for my family AND spend time with them.

I had found the solution to my problem.

However, lest you think I'm a genius, my solution to passive income was not real estate—it was a pizza franchise.

My Transition to Becoming a Full-Time Entrepreneur

By this time, I had some money invested in a franchise development company. During the company's Christmas party, I met a few of the Five Guys Burgers franchisees (Five Guys Burgers & Fries is one of the hottest burger franchises that started in Northern Virginia). They told me they were hiring an experienced multi-unit restaurant operator who would run the business, they would fund it, and count the passive income.

Bingo! That's exactly what I wanted: passive income. Because the Five Guys Burgers franchise was no longer available in my area, I went with the next best thing: an up-and-coming pizza franchise.

I was going to bet big on passive income. My plan was to deploy my entire net worth into this pizza franchise. I thought I had enough to fund three to five restaurants, which would then cover my living expenses and fund additional units. I had a 20-unit plan, and I set the plan in motion.

I hired an experienced restaurant operator, signed a franchise agreement and lease, and opened my first pizza restaurant in April 2006. Within the next six months, I had bought out another franchisee, turned his store around, and built and opened our third location. Over the next twelve months, I built one more restaurant and bought another two, and I increased sales between 25% and 50% in just a few months.

It turned out I was pretty good at this.

And then the recession hit.

Sales plummeted, and two stores began losing money. I had no choice but to sell both locations at the worst time in history to sell ANYTHING, especially restaurants that were losing money.

Welcome to entrepreneurship, Michael!

By 2009, things had stabilized, but by 2013 I realized that our profit margins had been slowly shrinking, and I could no longer afford my multi-unit restaurant operator. With a heavy heart, I had to let him go and manage the restaurants myself. That was not something I had planned for or even wanted. So much for passive income!

Despite my best efforts to turn things around, the slow downward grind continued, and nothing I did made a difference. I decided to sell all of the restaurants, but I didn't realize how long that would take. It took me nearly two years to sell all of them, and at rock-bottom, all-cash prices. A restaurant that cost $300,000 to open sold for all cash for around $40,000.

It was gut-wrenching.

What was worse was the ever-increasing negative cash flow. I was losing $10,000 a month and exhausting all possible lines of credits. I estimate that I was three months away from losing everything. Fortunately, I sold the first restaurant, and then a second, which cut the bleeding and put some money in my pocket to extend the runway.

This particular experiment, while educational, cost me nearly everything.

During this time, I was also searching for the perfect investment on the real estate side.

After reading *Rich Dad Poor Dad* in 2004, I had decided to dabble in real estate investing. I had signed up with a local wholesaling mentor, who taught me how to market for deals. After my first postcard campaign, I acquired two deals from the same out-of-state owner. Within six months, I had renovated and re-sold those two properties for a $110,000 profit. By working part-time on these two house flips, I made as much as my entire salary at the software company.

It blew my mind. *Still, I knew that the real money was in commercial real estate.*

I continued to flip a few more houses, but everything was pointing to apartment buildings as a way to create passive income and long-term wealth. In 2007, I attended a boot camp and immediately started calling brokers in Texas and sending letters to property owners. I educated myself. I developed financial models. I analyzed deals. I called property managers and lenders.

After nine months of activity, I finally got a verbal agreement on an 82-unit property in College Station, Texas. By this point, I had probably looked at 120 deals, so I knew it was a good deal. It was a light value-add opportunity. It needed some landscaping and TLC, but most importantly, the rents were about $125 under market and expenses were high. The property manager felt very confident about making this property shine.

The problem was, I was building and buying restaurants. I knew that if I did this deal, I would have to travel to Texas and spend some time there. I couldn't do both. After some deliberation, I decided to put the whole real estate thing on hold to focus on the restaurants.

You Can Make Great Money Flipping Houses

By 2009, the dust had settled: I sold my two restaurants at a massive loss but stopped the bleeding. Operations (and profits) stabilized on the other four locations. My life consisted of meeting with my operator once per week and counting the passive income that was comfortably covering my living expenses.

I had become financially free!

This allowed me to revisit my interest in real estate, and I decided I wanted to flip houses as a business. There was a huge supply of foreclosures, but at the same time, the retail market was recovering rapidly. This meant I could buy a house for $80K, put in $35K, and sell it for $185K. My original plan was to get back into apartment building investing, but this opportunity was too big to pass up.

My biggest problem was that I had no more money.

I had deployed my entire net worth into the restaurants. I'm not complaining, because at the time, they were generating the passive income I had desired. There just wasn't any cash left to invest in houses. I thought that perhaps I could convince some friends to invest. I proposed a $25K loan with 12% interest, and my father-in-law and brother-in-law were the first to bite. I then recruited a friend.

That's when I had a huge AHA moment:

<u>My ability to scale this business is only limited by my ability to find deals and raise money—not by my (lack of) financial resources.</u>

Over the next three years, I raised a million dollars and flipped over thirty houses. And I made good money, too.

But there was another problem: flipping houses was a TON of work!

I realized that if I wasn't buying, fixing, or selling a house, I wasn't going to make money. There was never any residual income after selling a house. It felt like a full-time job, and I was burning out. I then thought about building up a portfolio of single-family houses instead of flipping them. But then I discovered a second problem: I wasn't going to be able to replace my income with single-family rentals.

One day I sat down at my kitchen counter and put pen to paper to try to figure out how many houses I would need to own to replace my income. My goal was $10,000 per month. I felt that if I bought right, I could get each rental to cash flow $200 per month. At that rate, I would need at least fifty houses in my portfolio.

Fifty rentals? How long would THAT take? *A long time!*

How much work would that be? *A lot of work!*

That's when I remembered my apartment building training back in 2007, and I realized that investing in apartment buildings had several major advantages over single-family houses.

6 Reasons Apartment Buildings Are Better Than Single-Family Houses

I discovered six reasons that made apartment buildings superior to single-family house investing:

#1: Apartment Building Investing is More Passive

Unless an investor has a large portfolio of houses, it's not common to have a property manager manage the houses. I found that most of the time, investors were self-managing their houses.

On the other hand, with apartment buildings, professional property management is *built into the business model.* Once I found a good property manager, he or she would find and pre-screen the tenants, answer phone calls in the middle of the night and handle repairs, collect the rent, and track all of this with reports that I could review.

The passive nature of apartment building investing appealed to me over the more active work of single-family house investing.

#2: You Can Control the Value of an Apartment Building

I knew that the value of single-family houses was determined by what other houses in the same area sold for in the last six to twelve months. Even with a rental property, if one got a little more rent than the other, it would be valued about the same, all things being equal.

With apartment buildings, and commercial real estate in general, it's different. It's much less about comps and much more about how much net income the property produces. The more income it produces, the higher the value. I could have two identical buildings next to each other, and one could be worth more because it produces a higher net income than the other.

The implications of this are enormous: I could buy an underperforming building, perhaps one whose rents are low, expenses are high, and I could increase the income and decrease the expenses (perhaps by the use of a professional manager). As a result of those efforts, the property could be worth substantially more than before. It didn't depend on how much the building down the road sold for; it was solely dependent on how much net income it was producing.

With apartments, I wasn't dependent as much on market forces I couldn't control; instead, I could control the value by influencing the net income it could produce.

#3: Apartments Are Less Risky Than Houses

According to the Housing Finance Policy Center 2015 Chartbook, the Freddie Mac delinquencies peaked for single-family houses at about 4% in late 2009 (FHA delinquencies was even higher at 9%).

At the same time, delinquencies for multifamily properties peaked at 0.4%, and that included the hardest-hit areas (California, Arizona, and Florida). In other words, multifamily delinquency rates were 90% lower than the residential rate during the worst economic downturn since the Great Depression. This might explain the next point.

#4: You Can Get Cheap and Unlimited Financing

Because of the recession, there were now limits to how many houses someone could finance with bank loans. Through long-term banking relationships, some investors were getting around that through commercial loans. But they were almost always personally guaranteed—meaning, if they lost a house, the bank could go after their personal assets.

But banks were lining up to fund apartment buildings. The interest rates were incredibly low, and in many cases, you could get *nonrecourse loans*, which means they didn't have to be personally guaranteed. Best of all, there was no limit to how many loans you could have … the sky was the limit.

#5: You Can Get Paid for "Syndicating" Apartment Building Deals

Syndication is the process of finding deals, raising the down payment from private investors, and putting the deal together. What I discovered is that syndicators get paid for doing this in three ways:

- **Upfront.** Syndicators can get paid when they purchase a property with an *acquisition fee*, which can range from 1% to 5% of the purchase price. The acquisition fee is compensation for all the work the syndicator has done up to this point—including looking at dozens of deals that didn't work out, negotiating and closing this deal, finding the investors, risking the down payment, and organizing the whole thing. Without the syndicator, there would be no deal.

- **While they own the asset.** The syndicator gets "sweat" equity in the deal, typically, from 10% to 30%. They are sometimes also paid an *asset management fee*, which is a percentage of net income.

- **When they sell or refinance the asset.** The syndicator can be paid a "capital transaction" or "disposition" fee (1%–3% of the sales price) when they sell the asset.

I discovered that I could be compensated and build my portfolio just by syndicating deals!

Please watch my video *How to Pay Yourself $30,000 When Buying an Apartment Building with Investors* in the Companion Course to see how I analyze a deal to come up with acceptable sponsor fees. Go to FinancialFreedomTheBook.com/course > Chapter 1: My Rocky Road to Financial Freedom.

#6: Apartments Are More Scalable

When I revisited my goal of achieving $10,000 of passive income per month, I determined that I might need to syndicate and control about one hundred units. Rather than buying fifty single-family houses (which would take a lot of work and time), I could probably control one hundred units in just a handful of deals in the next three to five years. At that point, I could quit and sit on the beach, or I could just keep going and build a legacy I could pass on to my children.

Of all the businesses I had done—software, flipping, rentals, short sale negotiation, options trading, and restaurants—only apartment buildings had a unique combination of passive income, control, favorable risk profile, availability of financing, and scalability.

The New Plan

From that point forward, my plan was to focus only on apartment buildings. I dusted off the old apartment building books and began looking for deals in the DC area, where I had flipped three dozen houses. This new plan had to work because my restaurants were losing money, and I had no other source of income. And going back to a regular job was unacceptable to me. There was no Plan B, and I knew I had to make it work.

But I had two problems: I didn't have any money to invest, and I didn't have the experience. Despite my house flipping resume, brokers and sellers weren't taking me seriously because I hadn't done a multifamily deal before. It was frustrating, and I felt stuck.

I thought I needed a ton of money to get started, but then I discovered that I could raise it from private individuals, and they were GLAD I asked them to invest. I then discovered some tricks that encouraged brokers to take me seriously and ask me about my track record. And I'm going to share these tricks with you.

In 2011, one of my wholesalers contacted me about a 12-unit apartment building in Washington, DC, he had under contract. It was listed by one of his residential realtors, and he thought I should take a look at it. I ended up closing on the deal—with none of my own money.

Let me share with you how that first (small) deal made me $40,000 per year so that you can understand the power of apartment buildings.

CHAPTER 2

The First Step to Financial Freedom

I'm going to use my first deal as an example to demonstrate to you *with real numbers* how powerful apartment building investing can be. And best of all, I didn't use any of my own money. Let me show you exactly how this deal added $40K to my net worth every year for five years, and I hope in the process you'll see that you, too, can do a deal like this.

Here's how I bought the property:

- **Source:** MLS (listed by residential broker)
- **Purchase Price:** $530,000
- **Renovations:** $54,000 (or $4,500 per unit)—it needed a lot of renovation
- **Cash Needed to Close:** $227,000 raised from 5 investors in return for a 50/50 split
- **Projected Returns:** 15% per year for the investors
- **Acquisition Fee:** $15,900 payable to me at closing
- **Business Plan:** Raise rents from $595 to $825 over the next 5 years and then sell

After closing on the property, I renovated the exterior of the building and many of the units. This allowed me to slowly raise the rents, fill the vacancies, and evict nonpaying tenants. After five years, I had it under contract to sell for $850,000. Overall, this building made me a profit of $198,434 in five years, or about $40,000 per year.

How is it possible to make $40,000 per year with such a small building and with none of my own money in the deal?

Let me break it down for you by profit center:

- **Cash Flow:** Over 5 years, the cash flow was a total of $130,545 (after all expenses and my fees). That's about $181 per unit per month. Cash flow was tight the first couple of years, but it picked up in the last 3 years (as we raised the average rent from $595 to $825).

- **Appreciation:** The profit from appreciation was $146,500 after closing and sales costs.

- **Loan Reduction:** The loan principal was reduced by $48,265 in 5 years.

The total profit from cash flow, appreciation, and loan reduction was $325,310. Since I had a 50% share, my portion of the profits was $162,655.

What about the $15,900 acquisition fees that I pay myself at closing?

Oh, I almost forgot ...

I paid myself $15,900 at closing when I bought the building. I also charged an asset management fee of $2,275 per year (1% of money raised) and a 1% disposition fee of $8,500 when we sold the building.

All told, my sponsor fees totaled $35,779 for a total profit of $198,434, or about $40,000 per year.

It wasn't rocket science. And you can do this too.

What did I really do with this property?

I found a property with some problems that I felt I could fix in three to five years by using a professional management company. I renovated the property, increased the rents, and reduced the vacancy. It wasn't rocket science. It required some knowledge, taking action, and hiring the right property management company to execute on the plan.

> If you'd like to see another case study of the power of commercial real estate, then watch my video *How to Use Commercial Real Estate to Add $1M to Your Net Worth in 5 Years* in the Companion Course.
>
> Go to FinancialFreedomTheBook.com/course > Chapter 2: The First Step to Financial Freedom.

If you feel a bit overwhelmed by the numbers, just take a deep breath. Make sure you don't miss the main point here: *Apartment buildings (even smaller ones) are the single best way to create passive income and long-term wealth so you can do whatever you want in three to five years.*

That first deal changed my life forever because it set me on the path of financial freedom that I was seeking. Today I'm a full-time entrepreneur, investor, and coach, and I'm passionate about helping others become financially free in three to five years by investing in apartment building deals with a special focus on raising money.

Today, my partners and I control over $24 million in performing multifamily assets all over the United States. In addition to investing nationwide, I teach others how to do their first apartment building deal through content on my website, www.TheMichaelBlank.com, as well as through additional training programs.

I've helped students acquire over 750 units valued in excess of $27M, and we're on track to do 1,000 units in the next twelve months through our unique coaching and "Deal Desk" program. I'm the host of the popular podcast Apartment Building Investing with Michael Blank, and I write regularly for Bigger Pockets and Flipnerd's REI Classroom.

I work when I want to, and I can be with my kids during the day. I take my wife out to lunch several times a week. We also homeschool our kids; combined with the passive income from real estate, that allows our family to travel quite a bit. When we travel, we spend a month or two in whatever destination we choose.

But I gotta tell you: I'm pretty frustrated with my own journey to financial freedom. It took too long and cost me too much money. And it's all because of the false beliefs I had about apartments.

Most real estate investors never become financially free because they think they can do it with single-family house investing, *but they usually can't*. And they dismiss investing in apartments because they think it's an advanced strategy for which they need years of experience and tons of money.

As it turns out, you don't need experience or your own money.

It gets even better than that.

Not only do you *not* need experience or your own money, from the time you decide to pursue a multifamily investing strategy, you will be three to five years away from replacing your income.

It's all because of the curious "Law of the First Deal."

The Curious "Law of the First Deal"

I've interviewed dozens of successful real estate investors on my podcast who were either financially free or almost there. And I noticed their path followed a very specific and consistent pattern, which went like this:

- Their first deal was the smallest; it was the hardest to do, and it took the longest.
- The second and third deal followed in rapid, almost automatic succession.
- By the third deal, they had replaced their income.
- It didn't matter how big the first deal was.
- They achieved financial freedom within two to three years of *deciding* they were going to pursue a multifamily strategy.

This pattern is so consistent that I call this phenomenon "The Law of the First Deal," which can be stated as follows:

The first multifamily deal (of ANY size) results in financial freedom within three to five years.

That's how powerful that first multifamily deal is.

Don't believe me?

Take a look at these entrepreneurs who have replaced their income with apartment buildings in under three years:

"It Took Me Two Years to Replace My Income"

I'll let Brad Tacia tell his story about how he replaced his income with passive apartment building income less than two years after deciding to pursue a multifamily investing strategy. You remember the beginning of Brad's story: He planned to buy ten single-family house rentals and replace his income in ten years, but actually ended up buying five rentals over five years. Brad picks up the story from where we left off.

> I had heard about multifamily and started to look into it in early 2015. I got some training, read some books, and started analyzing deals and making offers. I didn't have any previous apartment experience, and I didn't feel like I was ready, but I just did it anyway.
>
> About eight months later, I had my first deal under contract, a 12-unit in Monroe, Michigan, about an hour from where I lived. For the down payment, I made an early withdrawal from my IRA and used a bank loan for the rest. Almost six months after closing on that deal, I purchased the 12-unit next door with a partner. Four months after that second deal, I closed on a 63-unit with a different partner.
>
> After that, I had covered my living expenses with passive

income from the apartment buildings—just under two years after I decided to pursue multifamily.

In early 2017, I quit my job.

My life has been so much better since I left my full-time job. I am able to get more sleep, exercise more, and do all sorts of things that I have been putting on the back burner because I didn't have enough time. Most importantly, I have been able to spend a lot more time with my family. My relationship with my wife and kids has improved dramatically. I find that I'm able to think more strategically about my life.

Since replacing my income, I have not stopped investing in apartment buildings because I enjoy the activity, and it's a great way to build generational wealth. I bought a 23-unit with yet another partner, and then I syndicated a 50-unit deal. Today I control a total of 160 units, and I don't plan on stopping.

That first deal was like a giant domino for me. It was the hardest to do, and of all the deals it took the longest. I didn't really know what I was doing; I didn't have a track record. I had to overcome a lot of obstacles.

But that first deal enabled the financial freedom I have now.

Once I did that first deal, the second and third came almost automatically, and they kept getting bigger. In less than two years from when I started investing in multifamily apartments, I had covered my living expenses through passive income.

I'm excited about helping other people become financially free like me. That's why I joined Michael's program as a coach, so I could help students do their first deal. I know that once they do that first deal, the second and third deals will follow quickly, and they will have replaced their income. That's what I'm excited about.

"Twelve Months to Quit My Job!"

Drew Kniffin recounts his journey from W-2 job to retirement in just twelve months after deciding to get started with apartment buildings.

> I became the accidental landlord in 2008 because I couldn't sell my condo, and so I rented it out. I didn't do anything with real estate for five years, until I realized I didn't want to work for the rest of my life. I decided to pursue real estate, and guess what? That's right, I started with single-family houses. I bought a rental house out of foreclosure.
>
> I then realized that it would take WAY too long to quit my job, and New Year's Eve 2014 I decided to pursue multifamily investing. In early 2015, I purchased Michael's program and began to analyze deals and make offers. Three months later, I closed my first small apartment building, a 3-unit in Minneapolis, with two partners. I rehabbed the property and later refinanced it to fund some of my deals later in the year.
>
> And then the deals (and money) kept coming: a month later, I bought a 4-plex with a partner. Two months later, I bought a 32-unit property with two partners; half of the down payment was from the refinance of the triplex I bought earlier in the year.
>
> I stopped working my W-2 job twelve months after deciding I would pursue multifamily investing.

Since then I've done seven additional deals, and I now own 295 units in total. I just did a 62-unit deal and syndicated a 171-unit deal. Syndication is such a rush ... the sky is the limit!

That first deal is so critical. It's like riding a bicycle. It takes some effort at first to learn the skill, but once you have it, you can go so much further than you ever could before. The first deal was the hardest (even though it was small) and the second and third happened almost automatically. It's all about the first deal!

My life today would have been hard to imagine just two years ago. I can play with my daughter in the middle of the afternoon. I can go on trips without having to get permission from a boss (and do so often!). My outlook on my life and my plans are changing almost daily because I don't have to worry about working.

The freedom from investing in apartment buildings has changed my life so radically that it's hard to explain. All I know for now is that I want to help other people do the same thing I have done, and I believe that apartment buildings is the BEST way to do that. That's why I joined Michael's coaching staff, so that I could help as many people as possible do their first deal.

Tyler Sheff Covers His Living Expenses in Just Eleven Months

Like so many people seeking financial freedom with real estate, Tyler Sheff started by flipping houses.

And he was pretty good at it.

The problem was that he lived large and didn't account for the tax bill, which was so big that he was forced to get a job.

After several years of working for the government as a merchant mariner, he went from a five-figure to a six-figure income. But again, he was paying a TON of taxes. He also realized that he was missing his wife and two young kids because he was deployed for weeks and months on end. Something had to change, and soon. There was no way he could keep doing what he was doing.

His solution to the taxation and time problems was real estate. Together with his wife, they decided that this time around (he calls it "Act 2") it would be buy-and-hold real estate. And it would *not* be single-family houses but small apartment buildings because he didn't think he could cover his living expenses fast enough with single-family house rentals.

With that decision, Tyler took massive action.

He took a six-month leave of absence from the government with the goal of covering his living expenses with apartment buildings. The first thing he did was to apply the Dave Ramsey method of eliminating debt and reducing expenses.

He then found a half vacant 4-unit building and decided to use his VA loan to purchase it—with no money down! He renovated the two vacant units and moved his young family into one of them while he rented out the other three. He says he was clearing about $700 per month while living there for free. He then discovered vacation rentals and was able to increase cash flow to $4,000 per month—while his family still lived there!

He knew he could only use his VA loan once, but he didn't have any cash to buy more apartment buildings. So he decided he would try to raise money from others. He attended a money-raising seminar and came back armed and dangerous. He took his one-deal track record and started searching for buildings in Memphis. In rapid succession, he found two buildings, a 10-unit and 12-unit, and bought them with the help of his new investors.

He was living "for free" in the 4-plex, he had substantially reduced his living expenses, and he had passive income coming in from his 26 units, all with zero money out of his pocket. Nevertheless, he was nervous about cutting the cord with his W-2 job.

What if he'd just been lucky? What if things went wrong?

After some time, he overcame his doubts and fears and decided to quit his job to focus full-time on investing.

Elapsed time? Eleven months from the time he started his leave of absence.

That is the power of the Law of the First Deal: once Tyler did his first deal, the second and third followed in rapid, almost automatic succession, and he was able to cover his living expenses in just eleven months from the time he got started.

Once he was no longer working full time, Tyler was able to think about what else there is to do besides working all day every day. Today he is educating people about passive income from real estate through his Cash Flow Guys podcast and online material.

All because of the Law of the First Deal.

It Took Jay B. Two Years to Buy His First Duplex, but Then This Happened

Jay B. initially began looking into real estate to provide financial security for his family in case something happened to his job and to reduce his W-2 taxes. He has five kids and wanted to be a good mentor to them. He wanted to show them that they don't have to be stuck in a commuting job for thirty years like he was. He wanted to teach them how to be entrepreneurs, property owners, and to be the bank. One of his daughters has a learning disability, and he needed a way to provide for her long term. He also wanted to travel more.

The more he researched real estate, the more he came to the conclusion that multifamily was the way to go. But he wanted to start small. So he looked into duplexes. A lot of duplexes. Jay says that he looked at about 200 duplexes over two years before he finally pulled the trigger. He just wanted to be sure, and he had to overcome a lot of anxiety.

He self-managed that duplex for a while but then realized he didn't want to be in the management business. He needed to purchase larger buildings in order to have a professional management company do everything for him. His main problem was lack of capital, and so he started to talk with friends and family about investing with him.

By the time he closed on the duplex, he had an off-market, 36-unit deal in Phoenix, Arizona, under contract. It was mismanaged and was breaking even. He hired a professional manager and began increasing the income so that he could refinance and repay his investors.

Jay is a perfect example of the power of the first deal. It took him two years to do his first deal, and then it was only a duplex. But then an interesting thing happened. The second deal followed in rapid, almost automatic succession. And I'm sure Jay will do his third deal in just a few months, and then he'll be out of the rat race forever.

This is the power of the Law of the First Deal in action.

"I'm About to Quit My Truck Driver Job"

Brooks Everline is a UPS driver during the day and decided that he didn't want to do that for the rest of his life and was looking for a way out. After exploring various options, he decided that multifamily investing would be the way to go, but with his limited resources, he knew he had to start small. So he decided to look for small apartment buildings.

He educated himself and then started to look for deals. He finally purchased a vacant 4-plex in Hagerstown, Maryland, with a hard-money loan, fixed it up, and filled it with tenants. The building cash-flowed $800 per month. He refinanced it to repay the lender.

Within three months, he closed on a second deal, a 5-unit building that now cash flows $1,000 per month.

How much does he need to quit his job?

Brooks needs $4,000 a month, so he's about halfway there.

And he's close to getting a 10-unit under contract.

Brooks is very confident that he'll be able to quit his job and become a full-time investor within the next twelve months.

Do you see how important that first deal is?

Even if it's "only" a duplex or quad?

$40,000 Per Month in Passive Income with Three Deals in Two Years

Shortly after deciding he wanted to replace his income from his financial management job, Bruce Fraser completed my training program. Three months later, he had his first deal under contract, a 138-unit in the Dallas/Fort Worth area. It took him nearly six months to close that deal, but once he did, it gave him $8,000 a month in passive income. Three months later, he had a 110-unit under contract and closed it three months later. That added $4,000 a month to his income. Six months after that, he closed his third deal, an 80-unit deal not far from his first deal, which now replaced his income from his previous job.

Total elapsed time? Two years from the time he decided to pursue apartment buildings.

Israeli Immigrant Replaces His Income in Under Three Years

Joseph Gozlan's story defines the word "grit." Once he decided that multifamily was the route he wanted to take, Joseph continued to drive through every challenge, getting creative and doing whatever it took to secure his first deal, despite the roadblocks and frustrations in his path. Two and a half years later, he's done two apartment buildings totaling 124 units, and he has five properties in the pipeline. Joseph's living expenses were covered, and he transitioned into full-time real estate in January 2018.

Joseph got his start in real estate back in 2005, when he and his new wife realized that their new five-bedroom home was too big for just the two of them, so they chose to stay in an apartment and rent the property. Two years later, they moved to the United States from Israel and recognized the opportunity provided by the market collapse. The Gozlans secured their real estate licenses and began actively hunting for deals, purchasing a duplex and several single-family homes.

He was struggling with his duplex, though, having to write a series of checks totaling $40,000 to repair foundation issues he discovered after closing (ouch!). In addition to wiping out any cash flow, he realized that he couldn't scale single-family homes quickly enough and something had to change. In early 2015, after several weeks of researching multifamily investing, he decided to shift his strategy.

His enthusiasm quickly subsided when he discovered that brokers weren't returning his phone calls. Joseph persisted and decided to source deals himself by sending out letters and postcards directly to apartment owners. After many months of frustration, he built rapport with the owner of a 22-unit apartment building who agreed to sell the building with seller financing. He closed on the property two long years after having decided to pursue a multifamily strategy.

The duplex had grown in value over the years, and he was able to refinance it to afford the down payment. He hired a professional management company, and over the next year he was able to increase the value of the building by $600,000.

Within just six months, he closed on a 102-unit property. After closing the first deal, everything became easier. After learning that Joseph was a "closer," brokers returned his phone calls. Investors were eager to talk with him. He had his team in place, and he was familiar with rent levels and expenses. So when his property management company told him about this off-market deal, he was able to act on it quickly. In forty-five stressful days, he managed to raise $1.4M from investors. When I interviewed him in Podcast #78, he was already under contract for a 28-unit and was working on five other off-market deals.

Together with the first deal, the 102-unit property was enough to cover Joseph's living expenses—about two and a half years after getting started with apartment buildings.

Financial freedom—and all because of the Law of the First Deal.

The ONE Thing for Achieving Financial Freedom with Real Estate

Gary Keller, in his excellent book *The One Thing* suggests that the key to achieving your strategic goals is to focus on ONE thing. The key question to ask to determine that ONE thing is this:

"What is the ONE THING, that if you could achieve it, would make everything else easier or even unnecessary?"

With regard to becoming financially free with real estate, the ONE thing is clearly and undoubtedly:

Your first deal.

That's it. If you remember nothing else from reading this book, then remember this one thing:

Focus on your first deal. Nothing else matters.

Forget everything else for the moment. Focus only on doing your first deal. Do whatever it takes. That's how important that first deal is.

That's why this book and all of my content and programs are focused on getting that first deal. I know that if I can help you do your first deal, you **will** be financially free in the next five years.

That is the power of the Law of the First Deal.

Now, you're probably thinking to yourself: *That's great, Michael, but I don't have the capital or experience to do what these people did, and certainly not in that time frame.* I thought the same thing, too, until I experienced the Law of the First Deal myself and started to study it.

In the next chapter, I'm going to reveal the 4 Secrets to Doing Your First Deal. Once you know these four secrets, there's nothing that will stop you from doing your first deal.

Nothing.

PART II

The 4 Secrets of the Successful Apartment Building Investor

CHAPTER 3

Secret #1: Raise All of the Money You Need to Do Your First Deal

When I first suggest the idea of buying apartment buildings as a means of achieving financial freedom, most people give me a weird look. By the expressions on their faces, I know they don't believe it's possible. And I can almost always predict what they'll say next. It will be something like …

"You need hundreds of thousands of dollars to do that, right?" (*You don't, actually.*)

"But I don't have any experience in real estate investing." (*Thankfully, you don't need any.*)

The truth is that you don't need thousands of dollars or experience in real estate investing to start investing in apartments. Did you notice that the entrepreneurs I introduced you to got started without a track record and, most of them, without any of their own capital? Yet two to three years later, they succeeded in replacing their income and quitting their jobs.

You want to know how they did it?

There are four secrets to apartment building investing success that will help you make your first deal and quit the rat race in the next two to three years—without prior experience or your own cash! This chapter is devoted to the first of these four secrets.

Secret #1: You Can Raise All of the Money You Need to Do Your First Deal

When I speak to people about starting with apartment buildings, the biggest objection I hear is that they don't have the capital. They tell me they'll start their investing career when they have money.

But who knows when that will happen?

And so they wait.

Or they'll say they can't see themselves putting a building under contract if they don't already have the funds in the bank. Who will take them seriously? How can they raise all of the money in time to close? And how can they get money from investors when they don't have a building under contract? It's a catch-22, so they're stuck.

You remember that when I saw a huge opportunity to flip houses, I had deployed all of my capital into the restaurants and had nothing left to invest. So I thought, *Shoot, maybe I'll see if some of my friends and family want to loan me money to fund these flips.*

I remember when I got my first commitment for $25K from a friend. I had this huge AHA moment when I realized that I could flip as many houses as I wanted if I raised the money from others. At one point, I had deployed about $1M, and we flipped about three dozen houses over the next four years. Since then, I've raised millions of dollars for restaurants and, of course, apartment buildings.

It turns out I didn't need my own money after all. And neither do you.

The truth is, you don't need tons of your own money or good credit to get started with apartment building investing. The solution to getting started now without having all the cash yourself is to raise money from private individuals.

Why You Should Raise Money from Others

Here are five reasons you should master the art of raising money:

1. **You don't need your own money.** I hate stating the obvious, but since the lack of money is the biggest objection to getting started with apartment investing, it deserves to be stated plainly. Just to reemphasize this point: if you raise money from investors, you don't need to use or have any of your own. DO NOT let this be the thing that keeps you from tapping into the best real estate strategy to achieving financial freedom.

2. **You can get more deals done.** Even if you have your own money to invest, there are only so many deals you can get done. On the other hand, if you are able to raise money from others, your ability to accumulate property is only limited by your ability to find good deals. The ability to raise money is an incredibly valuable skill to have.

3. **You can do bigger deals.** With the backing of investors, you can go after bigger and more lucrative deals than if you're just using your own funds.

4. **You have more eyes on the deal.** Richard Feynman, the famous physicist, once said, "The first principle is that you must not

fool yourself and you are the easiest person to fool."[1] When you're using your own money, no one else is looking over your shoulder, and you're more likely to make mistakes. If you can convince others to invest in your deal, chances are, you actually have a good deal.

5. **You're helping people.** People with money have two problems: (1) They're not getting a reasonable and consistent return, and (2) they're paying too many taxes on what they earn. You can solve both of these problems. You're connecting people with one of the safest investments on the planet (multifamily) that yields attractive returns and offers incredible tax benefits. Instead of being afraid to ask people for money, you should be confident in knowing that you're actually doing them a favor. Even though they might be skeptical at first, you'll find that they'll become grateful for the opportunity you're providing to them.

You should be aware, though, that there are a few downsides to raising money and having investors:

- **You now need to report to your "bosses."** Chances are, you'll have to report to your investors in one form or another. You may have to give updates and financial reports to your investors to keep them posted. This certainly is more work than if it were just you in the deal. On the other hand, analyzing the Profit and Loss (P&L) statements and sending out reports makes you pay more attention to the deal. You should analyze the reports even if there are no investors, but few of us have this kind of

---

1   "Richard P. Feynman Quotes," BrainyQuote.com, accessed January 3, 2018, www.brainyquote.com/quotes/richard_p_feynman_137642.

discipline, and as a result, we don't pay as much attention to the investment as we should.

- **You may lose some control.** You may not be able to make all of the decisions without a vote from your investors. As I'll discuss later, there are ways to mitigate this risk in how you structure the deal.

- **You won't get 100% of the profits.** That's true, but as the saying goes, 100% of nothing is still nothing. If you can own 100% of the building by using your own money, great! But if not, use investor money and get in the game!

All in all, the advantages of using other people's money far outweigh the disadvantages. This doesn't mean you shouldn't use as much creative financing as you can (especially seller financing). Bottom-line, if you get skilled at raising money from others, you can get started with real estate investing TODAY.

The Money is Out There

When I speak to an audience of real estate investors, I demonstrate how much money is out there. I ask people to raise their hand if they have at least $25K in cash or IRA funds to invest in real estate. In a crowd of one hundred people, half the people raise their hands. I then ask who has at least $50K, and a couple dozen keep their hands up. I then ask who has at least $100K to invest, and a handful keep their hands up.

Very quickly it becomes obvious to people that there is well over a million dollars in the room looking for deals.

Could you imagine yourself networking with these people and potentially partnering on deals that you find?

You betcha.

As of the first quarter in 2016, total retirement assets held in the United States hit $24.1 trillion,[2] yet according to a 2016 GOBankingRates survey, 69% of Americans have less than $1,000 in their savings accounts.[3]

That's why when you speak to people and ask them if they have money to invest, they'll often say no. But when you ask them if they have an IRA account, they say, "Of course I do … I have like $400K. Why do you ask?"

What most people *don't* know is that they can use their IRAs to invest with **you**. And they don't have to pay early withdrawal penalties to do so. Instead, they take advantage of the IRS tax code that allows them to "self-direct" their IRA investment. This means they can transfer their IRA accounts to a "self-directed IRA custodian" and then legally invest the money in almost anything they want: stocks and bonds, of course, but also in LLCs—such as your apartment building.

Become more familiar with self-directed IRAs and educate your potential investors. They'll be skeptical at first but will soon discover

---

2   John Sullivan, "401k Assets Hit $4.8 Trillion in First Quarter of 2016," 401KSpecialist.com, June 27, 2016, https://401kspecialistmag.com/401k-assets-hit-4-8-trillion-first-quarter-2016/.

3   Cameron Huddleston, "69% of Americans Have Less Than $1,000 in Savings," GoBankingRates.com, September 19, 2016, www.gobankingrates.com/saving-money/data-americans-savings/.

that using their IRAs to invest is not only *legal* but also one of the best ways to increase their returns and grow their retirement accounts.

By this point you might agree that it makes sense to raise money, and that the money is out there. But you have a problem, which goes something like this: "I don't have a deal under contract, so I can't go out and talk to investors."

Yes, that is a challenge.

Or "I have a deal under contract, but now I don't have enough time to find investors so that I can close."

That's also a challenge.

This catch-22 keeps most real estate investors on the sidelines. This frustrates me because it doesn't have to be this way. I'm going to share a secret with you that will let you raise money from private individuals long before you have a deal under contract. This means you can get started today, right now. The secret is so hidden that I've never heard it revealed anywhere else. The secret will stun you with its simplicity.

Okay, here it is ...

The Secret to Raising Money Revealed

The secret to getting financial commitments from your investors long before you have your first deal under contract is to ...

Make up a deal.

Huh?

You make up a deal by creating a "Sample Deal Package." This document contains everything about your fictitious deal, including photos, information about the building and area, actual financials, your business plan, and projected financials and returns. You will use this Sample Deal Package to speak with potential investors. You will even use it to build credibility with other professionals you're trying to recruit to your team—commercial real estate brokers, lenders, insurance agents, attorneys, etc.

The difference between a Sample Deal Package and a real one is that all the information about the deal is accurate (photos, location, financials, etc.), except that you don't have it under contract. The other difference is that your fictitious purchase price may be lower than the asking price so that you achieve the desired returns for the investors. In other words, you approach your potential investors with a deal package that looks like the real thing.

How to Create Your Sample Deal Package

You can create a Sample Deal Package yourself following a three-step process:

Step #1: Get the marketing package of a building for sale. The first step is to find a property that is being marketed for sale. This property should be about the same size and in the same area that you are looking for. It should have a good marketing package (i.e., it should have photos, financials, rent roll, unit mix, and maybe some information about the area and demographics).

There are a variety of websites that list apartment buildings for sale. Just do an online search. For the purposes of creating the Sample

Deal Package, I suggest you use LoopNet because it's free and easily searchable.

Go to www.loopnet.com, create a free account, log in, and search for properties that match your criteria. Sometimes you can just download the marketing and financial package. Other times you need to contact the broker and complete a nondisclosure agreement to get access to the financials.

Look for a property that has a marketing package with at least photos, financials, rent roll, and unit mix. It's a bonus if it has extra goodies, like demographic information or rental and sold comps.

Step #2: Create financial projections. The marketing package you downloaded should contain the actual and projected financials for the property. You'll need a financial model to create ten-year financial projections and the estimated returns for your investors. In your returns, incorporate cash flow, reduction in the loan principal, and any potential appreciation at resale.

You can create your own, or you can purchase my Syndicated Deal Analyzer to get the job done.

I discuss more about analyzing deals in Secret #3: How to Analyze Deals and Make Offers in 10 Minutes (page 83).

Once you have the ten-year financial projections and estimated investor returns, you can copy and paste them into the Sample Deal Package.

Step #3: Create the Sample Deal Package. Here's the outline of each of the sections in the Sample Deal Package:

Executive Summary. This short section (half to full page) contains a summary of the investor terms (preferred rate of return, equity, projected returns, minimum investment, the term of the investment), a description of the property, and an overview of the business plan (renovate and raise rents, exit strategy, etc.).

Property Information. This section contains a description of the property, some words about the area, and the unit mix. I also add the business plan for this property. For example, if we're going to renovate the units and make other cosmetic improvements to raise rents, that would go in this section.

Opportunity and Business Plan. This is where you outline the problem with the property and how you're going to solve it.

Don't worry if your financial projections aren't quite right or that you don't have all the information. The accuracy of the financials is less important. What's more important is that you have a good *story* to tell.

Describe the opportunity and business plan with the property: perhaps the rents are under market because of poor management. Your plan is to make some minor cosmetic upgrades (about $2,000 per unit) and put a professional management company in place. If you can do that, you can increase rents and realize the estimated returns.

Financials. This section contains the rent rolls and actual financials.

Projected Financials and Returns. This section contains the five-year and ten-year financial projections and the estimated returns for your investors.

About the Management Team. Here you have a short bio of yourself, as well as some of your team members, for example: your property manager, attorney, and CPA. If you have any other important partners, advisors, or mentors, list them here. This section gives you credibility as someone who will be able to put a deal together and close.

You can download a template of a Sample Deal Package in the Companion Course by going to FinancialFreedomTheBook.com/course > Chapter 3 > Lesson #1: Sample Deal Package Word Template.

So What? What difference does the Sample Deal Package make in your money-raising efforts? Here are the three biggest benefits:

1) *It allows you to better visualize your deal.* This is critical as you expand your own comfort zone with doing your first commercial real estate deal or doing bigger deals than before. Seeing the photos, visiting the property, and writing and talking about it make this deal real for you. The more real it seems to you, the more comfortable you become and the more confidently you can talk about it.

2) *It empowers you to get started now.* You can now schedule meetings with potential investors and say, "I don't have a deal right now, but when I do, it will look substantially like this," and then you show them the Sample Deal Package. It gives you something to talk about … today.

3) *It will allow you to get financial commitments from your investors long before you actually have a deal under contract.* By the time you get a building under contract, you've already primed your investors and received financial commitments based on a deal substantially similar to that in the Sample Deal Package. When you actually have a property under contract, you will send your investors the real Deal Package, confirm their commitment, and close on time.

Creating a Sample Deal Package allows you to get started NOW with apartment building investing. It allows you to better visualize your deal, gives you the confidence to make offers, and secures commitments from your investors long before you put your first property under contract so you can close on time.

The 6 Steps to Raising Private Money

Now that you know the Secret to Raising Private Money using the Sample Deal Package, follow these six steps to use that Sample Deal Package to get financial commitments from your investors *before* you put a deal under contract:

Step #1: Create a Mind Map of Your "Top 20"

The first step in the money-raising process is to create a list of people you know. Take a piece of paper and create bubbles for each social group you're a part of: family, friends, neighbors, coworkers, Boy Scouts, sports, hobbies, church/synagogue, etc. Then inside each bubble, write the name of every person you know in that social group. Many people don't think they know anyone who could help, but after doing this mind map exercise, they're surprised how many people are actually in their sphere of influence.

Now transfer that list of people into a spreadsheet so that you can track your activity with them. The goal here is *to become more intentional* with your relationships. That means whenever you speak to someone, you do so in a natural way, but when the opportunity arises, you may steer the conversation to apartment building investing.

The mind map helps you identify the first list of people to contact. Pick your "top 20" and begin to reach out to them.

Should you use money from friends and family for investing? You're afraid that friends and family won't talk to you again if a deal goes bad—but here's a compelling argument for why using their money works well. Read my opinion by going to the Companion Course at FinancialFreedomTheBook.com/course > Chapter 3 > Lesson #2: Why You Should Use Money from Friends and Family for Investing.

Now, how do you get these people to say yes?

Step #2: Talk to EVERYONE and Get a Series of YES's

Never discount anyone—tell everyone you know what you want to do, and you will be surprised at what will happen. Always follow up with a lead from someone you know. Even if that person will not invest, she may invest later, or she may be able to refer you to someone else.

Make sure you don't "discriminate." Often, it's impossible to tell who has money and who doesn't. It's amazing how much money seemingly "low-key" people have stashed away in their IRA accounts. Similarly, it's amazing how little money the flamboyant banker next door has to invest in anything besides his boat and second house.

Many newbie syndicators make the mistake of trying to get a potential investor's commitment to invest too early. I've seen too many eager syndicators approach their circle of influence like this:

"Hi, Frank! I'm getting into apartment building investing, and

> I'm looking for investors. The minimum investment is $25K, and you can get a 10%–15% return on your money. Are you interested?"

The problem with this approach is that it's too direct and will likely lead to a "no" that then becomes a dead-end. And you only have a finite number of people in your circle of influence. You don't want a series of dead-ends; you want your circle of influence to introduce you to as many new people as possible.

You want to EXPAND your circle of influence.

Instead of going for the close early on, try to get introduced to as many people as you can. Focus less on the money-raising part and more on building relationships. Here's what this conversation might sound like when you speak with a friend or acquaintance:

> "Hi, Frank. I'm getting into apartment building investing. I think it's really going to change the life of my family. Would you mind taking about five minutes with me to tell you more about it? I'd really like to hear your feedback!"

Your friend will probably reply, "Sure. Whatcha got going on?"

Now you have your first yes.

You might continue:

> "It's pretty cool. I'm looking for buildings with about fifteen units, and I'm going to buy it with investors. The minimum investment is $25,000 per investor, and they're getting a 10%–15% return per year on their money. They can invest with cash, of course, but also with their IRA or 401(k). Would

you happen to know someone who might be interested in a five-minute phone call to talk about this more? [Even if you don't think they have the money, they might know someone who does.] So at this point, I'm just looking for anyone you think might be interested in taking a phone call with me."

Your friend might say, "Yeah, I might be interested!" BINGO, another yes.

Or he might say, "Well, my boss might be. He's been talking about investing in real estate, and I think he bought a rental a little while ago."

You: "That's great. Would you feel comfortable asking him if he'd be interested in a five-minute phone call with me?"

Friend: "Sure, I don't think that would be a problem."

Another yes.

Instead of asking for any kind of financial commitment, all you're asking for is a five-minute phone call. Because these people presumably know and trust you (at least to some degree), they're more likely to introduce you to someone else they know who might be interested—even if they think that person doesn't have any money.

Remember: you want to expand your network and build relationships. That's your first priority; raising money comes later.

Always remember the following best practices:

- **Talk to everyone and don't discriminate.**
- **Always ask for referrals and follow up with them.**

- **Mention the minimum investment.** When you invite someone to that first meeting, you say what the minimum investment amount is. Otherwise, if you're looking for a minimum $50,000 and the person only has $10,000 to invest, you're wasting everyone's time. By the same token, if the other person accepts the meeting, they're implicitly saying they are capable of and potentially interested in investing at that level.

Once you feel it's appropriate, ask the person to meet with you to talk specifically about potentially investing with you.

Step #3: Ace Your First Investor Meeting

What do you want to accomplish with your first investor meeting? Ideally, you should get some level of financial commitment from your investor. But before you do, you must address their main concern.

Make sure you identify the main risk factors of your proposed deal and how you plan to mitigate them. If an investor hears that this is an "unbelievably safe investment without any real risks," they'll grow suspicious. You'll be much more credible if you're upfront about the risks and how you plan to address them.

Speaking of risk …

You have two strikes against you as far as the investor is concerned. First, he doesn't know and trust you (yet); and second, you probably don't have a track record (yet).

You will spend most of the meeting making the investor comfortable with you. Only then can you address other objections and discuss the deal itself (including how much money they'll make). Your goal in the meeting, then, is to build rapport with the investor and demonstrate to him that you will be successful, even though you don't have a portfolio of successful deals. You can do this by talking about where you were born, about your family, where you grew up and went to school. Sharing personal information like this will help you connect to your potential investor. Chances are you'll discover things you have in common.

Then describe your professional experience. Focus on your track record of success in whatever you have accomplished professionally, even if it's unrelated to real estate. Your investor should be able to see that you tend to succeed in whatever you do. If you had a failure, you can turn that into a strength by talking about what you learned.

Talk about your enthusiasm about buying apartment buildings. Why are you interested? What have you done so far?

Once you're done talking about yourself—try to keep it brief—it's time to talk about your team. It's all about your team.

Talk about the property manager you recruited who manages 5,000 units in the city and specializes in turn-around projects. Mention the real estate attorney who will be handling the closing, and your SEC attorney who will handle the syndication documents. Talk about any advisors or coaches on your team.

At this point, you've done most of the talking, but that's okay. You shared about your life and your passion about building long-term wealth for you and your investors with apartment buildings. You introduced your team. If you've done your job, your investor will say that he knows you a lot better and has become more comfortable with the prospect of working with you.

It's now time to shift the conversation to how you might do business together. That's where your Sample Deal Package comes in.

Here's your script:

> **You:** I have a deal for us to look at. I don't actually have this building under contract, but when I do have a deal, it will look substantially like this. I wanted to get your feedback on the terms and projected returns. Would that be okay?

> [Next, review the executive summary page of your Sample Deal Package with the investor, focusing specifically on the investor terms, not the deal itself (that comes a little later).]

> **You:** The deal I'm looking for should produce an average annual return of around 13% over the life of the investment. This will consist partly of cash flow each year, as well as appreciation. The minimum investment I'm looking for is $50,000. How interesting would that be to you?

> **Investor:** That would be interesting to me. How long would the money be locked up?

> **You:** I'm telling investors that they should be prepared to keep their money in for at least five years. This would allow us to build the value we're looking for. How would you feel about that?

> **Investor:** That would be fine. Would there be any cash flow distributions?

> **You:** Yes. Typically, we will pay out distributions once per quarter. How would that work for you?

Investor: That sounds reasonable. What do you see as the greatest risks?"

You: "It would depend on the deal, but in general, I think the greatest risk is our ability to execute our business plan. We could fall short of our projected returns, or it might take more time to achieve. For example, let's say our plan calls for the renovation of half of the units so that we can raise rents by 30%. We would make sure we have the money in the bank account to fund the renovations. However, maybe the tenants won't move out as quickly as we think, so it could take longer to raise the rents.

That said, my goal with the first few properties we buy will be to keep these kinds of risks to a minimum. In other words, I don't want a completely vacant building or a building with a lot of problems. I'm going to look for a good deal for a relatively stable building.

Once I have a building under contract, I will outline the plan in more detail and identify the risks so that you can make a better decision. Before we look at the Deal Package, what other questions or concerns do you have regarding the returns and terms we've talked about so far?

[At this point, the investor should be relatively comfortable with you as a person, as well as with the risks, returns, and terms of the investment. If you're just starting out talking with investors, don't make it sound like your terms are set in stone. Instead, gather information from your investors about what they would (and wouldn't) like if they were to invest with you.

Next, review the Sample Deal Package itself. Don't spend too much time though, because you probably don't have much left in the meeting anyway. Although the numbers aren't for a real deal, it should give the investor a feel for the kind of deal you're looking for.]

You: Let's take a few minutes and look at the Deal Package. Like I said before, this is not a deal I currently have under contract. But when I do, it will look a lot like this.

[Then briefly go through each section of the Deal Package just enough to orient the investor and answer any questions. Don't focus on the numbers since these will change.

Finally, you want to close by describing the logistics of closing on a deal from the investor's perspective:]

You: I appreciate your time today! Here's what will happen next. I'll keep you posted, and when I have a property under contract, I'll email you the Deal Package. If you're interested in investing, just let me know the amount you're considering, and I will reserve that amount. Once I get commitments from all of the investors and due diligence is satisfactory, I will instruct the attorney to begin the closing process.

You will receive an LLC Operating Agreement and a Private Placement Memorandum. You sign the Operating Agreement and a subscription agreement that documents the investment amount. A day or so before closing, you wire the funds to the closing attorney.

My goal will be to send an email report to the investors once per month in the beginning, and once things have stabilized, I will send out quarterly reports with any distributions.

What questions or concerns do you have about this?

Give them the Sample Deal Package to take home, and schedule a follow-up phone call or meeting to discuss any questions or concerns.

Don't skip this step! Make sure you address their concerns *now* while you still have time rather than waiting until you have a deal under contract and time is of the essence.

If you follow this process, you'll be amazed how quickly you can get commitments from your investors once you have a deal under contract. If you do this up front, it will give you the confidence to make offers on properties and secure the funds in time to close.

Step #4: Stay in Touch

After this first meeting, it's important that you stay in touch with the investor. Hopefully, you have the first follow-up call or meeting scheduled to discuss any questions or concerns they might have. Ask them again if they feel comfortable in moving forward if you found the right deal.

After that second meeting, it's very important to stay in touch with that investor since you don't know how long it will take until you have an actual deal. Call or send an email at least once a month; give an update and see what's new in his or her life.

One thing you might consider is putting all of your potential investors on an email list (like MailChimp) and sending out something like a newsletter every month. That way, they're used to hearing from you, and you've created a systematic way of staying in touch.

Step #5: Sign a "Letter of Intent to Invest"

Once an investor verbally commits to a certain dollar amount, I use something I call a "Letter of Intent to Invest." It's a short one-page document that is not legally binding but "formalizes" that commitment in writing. A nice additional benefit is that it can act as a "Proof of Funds" letter later when you're making offers.

You can download the Letter of Intent to Invest template in the Companion Course. Go to FinancialFreedomTheBook.com/course > Chapter 3 > Lesson #3: Letter of Intent to Invest (Template).

Step #6: Expand Your Network

Once you've contacted everyone in your immediate circle of influence (and you continue to cultivate those relationships), it's time to cast a wider net. Here are three tips to expand your network of potential investors:

- **Tip #1: Warm up your cold contacts.** Take a look at your contacts list in Gmail, Outlook, or whatever address book you use. Chances are, you have hundreds of contacts but have lost touch with most of them. Before you delete them, perhaps there's a way you can reconnect with your cold contacts.

  Import your cold contacts into a mail service program like MailChimp. Send out a first email and apologize for how bad you've been about staying in touch. Give them a general update about your life and ask what's new with them. You'll be surprised how many people are delighted to hear from you! Boom, a list of new warm contacts.

Continue interacting with those new contacts in a natural way (i.e., don't start asking them for money, but simply reconnect). This may take several weeks or even months. Be patient. For other contacts who didn't respond, continue sending out a monthly update. In future communications, you can be more intentional about your apartment building activities so that people begin to know you in that context.

Continue this process until a person unsubscribes from your newsletter or you become reconnected. A cheap and easy way to expand your network!

- **Tip #2: Network at local real estate events.** One of the best ways to meet potential investors is at your local REIA. You should attend every REIA in a reasonable driving distance from you. Also go to meetup.com and look for local real estate meetups. There are usually several in your area, and if there isn't one, then consider starting one. You should shoot for attending one networking event per week.

- **Tip #3: Network on Bigger Pockets.** Bigger Pockets is probably the largest online community of real estate investors. If you're a Pro member, you can search for members in your area and send them a personal message. Start an online conversation, meet them at your local meetup, or start a new group for members.

There is no shortage of ways you can meet new people. Be creative and consistent with meeting new people.

The Secret to Raising Money Is a Game Changer

What difference does all of this make to your ability to get started with apartment building investing?

It makes **all** the difference.

If you use my Secret to Raising Money and follow the steps I just outlined in this chapter, you can get verbal commitments from investors *before* you have your first deal under contract. Wouldn't that enable you to make offers with more confidence?

Of course. In fact, it would give you a LOT of confidence.

Imagine if you had five investors who committed to investing $50K with you if the deal resembles what you showed them in the Sample Deal Package. That's $250,000 behind you.

Wouldn't that make a difference in how you spoke with brokers and sellers?

And once you have a real deal under contract, wouldn't it take you only a few days to actually raise the money you need to close?

Yes, and yes.

Therein lies the power of the Secret to Raising Money. Use it to make offers with confidence. Use it to raise money in days.

Now you know how to raise all of the money you need to do your first deal. That leads us to the next secret: how to get your offers accepted even if you're a newbie and don't have Proof of Funds.

CHAPTER 4

Secret #2: Get Your Offer Accepted without Experience or Proof of Funds

One of the main objections people have to getting started with apartment building investing is that they don't have the necessary experience. They think they need years of single-family house investing first before they can "graduate" to multifamily.

When I had my first apartment building under contract, I had flipped over thirty houses. Even though the idea of buying a 12-unit building made me break out into a cold sweat at the time, I felt like I had a pretty good track record with real estate.

But when I spoke with brokers and investors, they still quizzed me about my multifamily investing experience. When I shared that this would be my first one but had flipped over thirty houses, they weren't impressed with my track record. It was as if I got absolutely no credit for my house flipping experience.

I got a similar reaction from commercial real estate brokers and other professionals I spoke to. They, too, gave me little credit for my single-family house investing and immediately honed in on my lack of multifamily investing track record.

I was stunned. I thought for sure my experience investing in single-family houses would set me up for multifamily investing, but it didn't. I think it's because in people's minds, single-family house investing is a completely different animal from multifamily.

I remember when I first started calling brokers in Texas. I had barely said a few words when the broker would ask me to send him a Proof of Funds along with my apartment investing resume. That usually ended the conversation, and the broker never returned another phone call.

Here's what I would say to a broker:

"Hi, my name is Michael, and I'm interested in purchasing multiunit properties around $1M with at least a 10% return. Can you send me some deals?"

It took me a while to figure out what was going on because I didn't know any better. I was making several mistakes that kept me from getting in the game.

The answer wasn't that I needed more experience. *I needed to prove my credibility.*

To teach you this second secret of how to get your offer accepted without experience or Proof of Funds, I need to show you how to avoid the common mistakes I fell into. I'm going to give you four tips to overcoming these mistakes so you will be taken seriously, even if you don't have **any** real estate experience.

Tip #1: Educate Yourself So You Don't Sound Like a Newbie

There's specific language that commercial real estate insiders use. Apparently, I wasn't using the right terms (or wasn't using them in the right way), and others immediately classified me as a newbie. The best way to avoid this mistake is to educate yourself. You must use the right language when you speak to other professionals, and you only have one chance to make a first impression. So if you call a broker and sound like a newbie, it will be difficult for you to convince him or her of your credibility.

You know you sound like a newbie when you get these questions from the broker:

- "The seller wants to see your Proof of Funds before I can send you the financials."
- "What multifamily experience do you have?"

Since I wasn't using the right language in my script when calling brokers, I wasn't proactively addressing the main concern every broker has when a new investor calls in: Would I be able close? Meaning, did I have the money and necessary experience? When I cold-called those brokers on the phone, that's what was going through their heads. They were trying to figure out if they should take me seriously or if I was wasting their time.

Here's a sample script that will keep you from sounding inexperienced:

"I work with a group of high net worth individuals, and we would like to expand into the Atlanta market. We already have property management company XYZ on board and are continuing to build our team. We're looking for deals in the $1M to $2.5M range with at least an 8% cap rate and are looking for stable value-add deals but no repositions. Is there anything you have in your pipeline that you can send over for me to review?"

Here's what you've done:

1. You addressed the money part by saying you're working with high net worth individuals.

2. You addressed the experience part because you're working with a property management company and say you're "expanding," implying that you already have experience.

3. You're using terms like *cap rate*, *stable value-add*, and *reposition*, which only commercial real estate insiders would use.

Do you see how a simple script change can make a huge difference? That's just one example of how education can pay off big for you.

So make sure you educate yourself! There is a lot of free material to get you started, but if you're serious, you're going to have to invest in your education. Here are some suggestions and resources to get you started:

- You can find a lot of free material. For example, all of my articles, videos, and podcasts on www.TheMichaelBlank.com are available to you at no cost.

- Be sure to access the Companion Course to this book, which contains additional material directly related to this discussion.

- Join Bigger Pockets and read every blog and forum post related to apartment building investing.

- Listen to every podcast related to apartment building investing.

- Read every book related to apartment building investing.

Once you've consumed all of the free stuff and you want to dive in deeper, then it may be time to invest in your education. Purchase an online course, attend a seminar, and/or hire a coach. You can see our offerings at www.TheMichaelBlank.com/products. Ours is just one approach; there are other quality courses and instructors out there. Look around, decide which one is the best fit for you, and then take action.

Tip #2: Build Your Team So You Don't Look Like a Newbie

The second mistake I made was not having a proper team behind me. When people asked who would manage the building, I couldn't answer because I hadn't hired a property management company yet. Investors asked me what attorney would be handling the transaction, and I didn't have one. Brokers were asking who my lender was, and I didn't have one of those either. None of this added to my credibility.

To avoid this mistake, surround yourself with people who have the experience you don't. If you have a strong team around you, then it's no longer about you (and your lack of experience) but more about the collective experience and track record of your team.

Imagine a conversation with a skeptical broker who asks you about your experience. With a strong team around you, you might be able to answer his questions like this:

You: Sure. I have Sam at XYZ property managers on board

who manages 4,000 units in town and specializes in the kind of value-add deals I'm looking for. Are you familiar with Sam?

Broker: Oh sure, great guy. He really knows what he's doing!

You: Yes, he really does. Mack Scibo is handling the closing logistics for me, and I'm working with Brandi at Coronado Bay for the loan.

Broker: I've done several transactions with Mack. He's very good and responsive. Brandi is out of Dallas, right?

You: That's right. She's also done several loans for one of the advisors I have on my team, Michael Blank.

WOW. Isn't that a considerably different conversation? Don't you think that would satisfy **anyone** who might be concerned about your lack of experience?

The first and most important team member to recruit is your property manager. He or she has the experience you don't and can give you instant credibility.

I alluded to an "advisory board." This can consist of one or more experienced multifamily investors who agree to be a resource to you. This could be an unpaid mentor or a paid coach. For example, if you decided to work with me as a coaching student, you would instantly have your first advisory board member. You can also find potential advisors at your local REIA, meetups, or by networking on Bigger Pockets.

Tip #3: Be Professional to Make a Good First Impression

You're not sounding like a newbie, and you have an experienced team around you. Now the third thing you can do to be taken seriously is to appear "professional."

This is not hard to do, and it will make a big difference. Here are a few things you can do to make a professional first impression:

- **Create an LLC.** It looks more professional if you're operating as a company and not as an individual. Pick a cool name and file the paperwork to register the LLC. You can normally do this yourself by researching online what's required in your state, and it's not expensive. In addition to looking more professional, you can also write off your business expenses.

- **Get business cards.** It just looks more professional if you can give someone a business card. It's easy and cheap to do this yourself. You can hire someone on Fiverr to design a logo for you and then use any of the online services available to design and print the business cards.

- **Create a website.** This is a bit harder if you're not much of a techie, but it's easier to do than ever before. Research other apartment building investors' websites and see which ones you like. I suggest creating a single page website to start, because it's easier and perfectly sufficient.

For step-by-step instructions on how to create your own website, please see the Companion Course. Go to FinancialFreedomTheBook.com/course > Chapter 4 > Lesson #1: Tips for Creating Your Syndication Website.

One note on the topic of looking professional: I've seen students get stuck in this step because they're perfectionists and are afraid to move on to the next step—making offers. I'd like to emphasize that this step is *optional!* You don't need business cards and a website to be taken seriously; they're just great tools to support your professional appearance. If you can knock these out in a week or two, great. But if this step is going to bog you down for weeks on end, then outsource or skip this tip.

Tip #4: Make Offers That Rock

My other big mistake was making offers that couldn't be taken seriously. The responses I got to my offers were mostly a request for my bio and Proof of Funds. I wasn't even invited into the game because I couldn't get past the gatekeeper.

Now that you've educated yourself, assembled an experienced team, and created a professional look, it's time to make an offer that gets the broker's attention.

Submitting a Letter of Intent (LOI) to make an offer is a good start, but it's not enough, especially when you're just starting out. It doesn't give you enough credibility, and it doesn't make your offer strong enough. Even if the broker now respects you as a potential buyer, he's going to have to present your offer to the seller. And if the seller isn't convinced you can close, they will not accept your offer, even if the price is higher than the other buyers.

When you make an offer, you want to put your best foot forward. The following components are essential for creating a strong Offer Package:

- **The Cover Letter**

  Start the Offer Package with a one-page Cover Letter that introduces you, your offer, and your extended team. My Sample Cover Letter also includes my updated bio that you can add to your board of advisors.

  > Download the Sample Cover Letter from the Companion Course. Go to FinancialFreedomTheBook.com/course > Chapter 4 > Lesson #2: Making Offers That Rock.

- **The Letter of Intent (LOI)**

  Follow the Cover Letter with the Letter of Intent, which contains the terms of your offer, such as price, down payment, and closing time line. This is used as the basis for negotiating the deal. Once you and the seller sign the LOI, you can forward it to your attorney to draft the purchase contract.

  > Download a Letter of Intent (Word Template) from the Companion Course. Go to FinancialFreedomTheBook.com/course > Chapter 4 > Lesson #2: Making Offers That Rock.

The Result: Instant Credibility with the People You Meet

When you follow these four tips, you're using the right language, you're talking about your team, and you're leaving a professional first impression. And you're putting it all together in an offer package that gets taken seriously.

Are you acting like a newbie?

No, not at all. You're acting like someone who knows what they're doing.

Are you going to lie about your lack of experience? No, not at all. You'll admit to it (if asked) and reference your team, your company, and your excitement about doing your first deal.

I can tell you that if you do these things, chances are very low that you'll ever be asked about your experience. This is because you just *appear* to have experience. And a broker is not going to risk offending you by asking you that question. What if you already owned hundreds of units? You might get pretty upset at the broker for having to justify the phone conversations you're having right now. Brokers are smart, and they're not going to risk upsetting a potential client.

You're probably thinking: *That's great, Michael. I can see how I can appear more experienced than I really am. But what if the broker asks me for Proof of Funds?*

What If I'm Asked for a Proof of Funds Letter?

The truth is, it is rare to be asked for Proof of Funds if you're using the right language and appear confident.

Philippe Schulligen had this to say when I asked him about his need for a Proof of Funds letter before he put his first deal under contract:

> *Michael, to answer your question, no, I have not been asked for Proof of Funds. Your course really boosted my confidence, and I used your scripts, so Proof of Funds never came up. I just had my first offer accepted for an 80-unit deal, and I'm negotiating the contract right now.*

Laura Guy reported that she struggled with the Proof of Funds question in the beginning:

> *I just got started with Michael and have made several offers. In the beginning, the brokers were giving me a hard time and were asking for Proof of Funds. But after several weeks, they stopped asking. In fact, I just had my first Letter of Intent accepted on a 53-unit deal. I'm excited about doing my first deal!*

You can tell that you sound like a newbie when you're getting these questions about track record and Proof of Funds. This is why educating yourself, developing your skills, and building your team is the key to being taken seriously by brokers and investors.

So the bottom-line is: if you sound and appear confident, the chances you'll be asked for a Proof of Funds letter are remote.

That said, it's normal to still be nervous about being asked. Not to worry. I'm going to show you three ways to handle a request for Proof of Funds when you don't have any.

3 Ways to Handle Requests for Proof of Funds When You Don't Have Any

The challenge is that if you're raising money, chances are, you don't have the net worth or liquidity to satisfy a seller's request for Proof of Funds. As a syndicator, you don't already have the funds sitting in a bank account. You're going to raise it from others and deposit the money into an escrow account for closing. But you don't have it right now.

This can be a real challenge to get a seller to ratify a contract with you. Sometimes the broker and/or seller want to see Proof of Funds (POF)—even if you do appear confident. This can be a major problem that you need to know how to address.

While showing the seller actual Proof of Funds would certainly satisfy them, there are other things you can do before you actually need to do that. Here are three tips you can follow when you get the request to show Proof of Funds:

Tip #1: Push back. A request for Proof of Funds signifies a lack of trust. If the seller knew for sure you were going to be able to close, they wouldn't ask you for this. The first thing you should do is push back with something like this:

> I understand you're concerned about our ability to close since we will be raising the money. But I already have the verbal commitment from my investors for the money we'll need to do the deal. It'll be in the escrow account when we close, but I don't have it in a bank account right now. So I can't give you Proof of Funds.
>
> But how about this? Why don't we get together and get to know each other? If you don't feel 100% comfortable moving forward with us, we'll part as friends. What do you say?

If you're feeling gutsy, you could add:

> If your seller insists on Proof of Funds, we're going to have to move on. I have another four deals I need to look at today.

People do business with people they like and trust.

The best way to build trust is with an in-person meeting with the broker and/or the seller. This gives you a chance to build rapport, tell them what you've done and what you want to do, and introduce them to the team members you have around you.

If you can't meet with the broker or seller in person, then you'll need to do it remotely with a phone call and email. If only email is possible, create a Cover Letter that provides an overview of your accomplishments and how you will be raising money to complete the deal. Include your bio and the investor package for this deal.

Do the best you can to make the seller comfortable with the idea of moving forward with you.

If Tip #1 fails and you still want to get into the deal, here are two more tips for you to satisfy the seller's request for Proof of Funds.

Tip #2: Demonstrate your investors' intent to invest. Another thing you can do shy of providing an actual Proof of Funds is offer the seller your Letters of Intent to invest (which we covered in "The 6 Steps to Raising Private Money"), signed by each of the investors that indicates the amount they are interested in investing. This often satisfies the seller, and to the investors, it's not legally binding in any way, and it doesn't cost them anything to sign it. However, it adds significant credibility to your cause.

Tip #3: Get Proof of Funds from one of your investors. If Tip #2 doesn't satisfy the obstinate seller and you're set on getting into the deal, there is yet a third option—to get one of your investors to give you Proof of Funds.

Proof of Funds can take different forms: It can be a bank or brokerage statement, or it can be a letter from the investor's banker or broker.

Many times, investors prefer the latter because it doesn't disclose exactly how much they have but confirms the amount that you need to show. If you want an example of such a letter, please access the Companion Course to download a template.

> Download the Bank Letter of Funds (Word Template) from the Companion Course. Go to FinancialFreedomTheBook.com/course > Chapter 4 > Lesson #2: Making Offers That Rock.

A Proof of Funds statement or letter doesn't cost the investor anything. It's not legally binding, and it doesn't require the investor to invest any money at all. So there is no obligation whatsoever on the part of the investor.

If you're struggling with getting a POF letter from one of your investors, you can pay $5.00 to get one from COGO Capital for up to $500,000 (more if you contact them). Search online for "COGO Capital Proof of Funds" to get the PDF letter. Sophisticated brokers will likely not accept this, but most of the time, the Proof of Funds letter is a formality or "checkbox" and will often do the trick. Another option is to join my Deal Maker's Mastermind that allows you to request a POF Letter from me.

Tip #4: Make the Proof of Funds conditional on a signed Letter of Intent. If you absolutely *must* provide Proof of Funds to move forward, then insist that it be conditional on a signed Letter of Intent. In your LOI, state that you will "provide Proof of Funds within 48 hours of ratifying the LOI." Explain to the broker or seller that you can get the Proof of Funds letter but that your investor wants to make sure the deal is real before they contact their financial institution to produce the letter. The best indication that deal is "real" is a signed Letter of Intent.

I hope that by now you see how these tips can make you appear more experienced than you really are. You've educated yourself so that you're using the right language. You've recruited a team that makes up for your own lack of experience and you talk about yourself in terms of that team. You've created a company and website, which makes a professional first impression. And you're leveraging all of this to make offers that will get accepted.

Now that we've addressed the issue of experience and lack of capital, let's look at the next critical skill you need, which is how to analyze deals and make offers. This may sound daunting, but I'm going to show you how to do in just ten minutes.

CHAPTER 5

Secret #3: How to Analyze Deals and Make Offers in 10 Minutes

Real estate is a numbers game. The more offers you make, the more deals you do. The problem is, analyzing apartment building deals can be time-consuming, which can limit your ability to make a lot of offers.

When I first got started back in 2007, I was completely overwhelmed. I would get a marketing package from a broker and enter the financials into a spreadsheet I had created to crunch numbers. Then I would make a few phone calls and do some research online.

It took me four hours to analyze a deal and make an offer. Four hours!

As you can imagine, I wasn't able to make a lot of offers; in fact, I nearly gave up because I was overwhelmed and couldn't get it done fast enough.

Back then I didn't have the tools or techniques I have now. Subsequently, I discovered a better way. I call it the "10-Minute Offer," and it will allow you to make an offer on a deal you get from a broker within ten minutes of getting the marketing package. It's that powerful, and it will accelerate the progress you'll make toward your first deal.

Now, just a word of warning: The 10-Minute Offer involves some numbers and simple math, but if you find your eyes glazing over, just keep reading. Even if you don't understand everything right now, just keep reading.

Okay, let's dive right into the 10-Minute Offer.

The 10-Minute Offer

Step #1: Adjust the Income—4 minutes

If the marketing package contains actual financials, look for the "Gross Scheduled Income." This is the income that should be collected if all units were occupied and rents were at market rent. Just use that number for the 10-Minute Offer.

Then look for the adjustments for vacancies, concessions, and bad debt, etc. If these adjustments are greater than 10%, then use that number, otherwise use 10% as a vacancy factor. If you only have the pro-forma financials (i.e., what the financials *should* be if the property were run efficiently), then use those numbers.

Your Adjusted Income is now the Gross Scheduled Income minus 10%.

Step #2: Adjust the Expenses—3 minutes

This is going to be easy. If the reported or pro-forma expenses are greater than 55% then use that number, otherwise use 55%. That will be your Adjusted Expenses.

Often, when the reported expenses are less than 55%, something is missing. For example, maybe the management fees are not included in the expenses because the current owner is managing the property on their own. Don't spend a lot of time analyzing this, but see if you can find some obvious expense that is missing from the broker's marketing package. You're going to use that as an argument that the expenses are unrealistically low.

Now you can calculate the Adjusted Net Operating Income:

Adjusted Net Operating Income (NOI) = Adjusted Income − Adjusted Expenses

Step #3: Use the Advertised Cap Rate to Come Up with a Revised Fair Market Value—3 Minutes

Usually, the marketing package advertises a certain Cap Rate for the property, or your broker will tell you what Cap Rate he or she used to determine the asking price. If the Cap Rate is not that obvious, you can quickly calculate it by using this formula:

Cap Rate = Net Operating Income / Asking Price

Make a note of that Cap Rate because you're going to use it to your advantage shortly.

If we have the Cap Rate and Net Operating Income, we can now calculate the Adjusted Value with this formula:

Adjusted Value = Adjusted Net Operating Income / Cap Rate

Here's an example. Let's assume the asking price is $653,000, the reported income is $95,000 and the expenses are $42,750. Once you apply the 10-Minute Offer technique, you get an Adjusted Value of $506,250 per the adjustments in the second column:

	Reported		Adjusted	
Gross Potential Income	$100,000		$100,000	
- Vacancies	($5,000)	5%	($10,000)	10%
= Income	$95,000		$90,000	
- Expenses	($42,750)	45%	($49,500)	55%
= NOI	$52,250		$40,500	
Cap Rate	8%		8%	
Value	$653,125		$506,250	

Typically, the Adjusted Value will be lower than the asking price because the income and expenses in the marketing package were overly optimistic to begin with! In this example, it's no different: the asking price is $653,000, but your adjusted value is $506,000 because the reported income was high, and the reported expenses were lower than our rule of thumb.

Make note of the adjusted price, and let's get back to the broker.

Step #4: Get Back to the Broker with Your Analysis and Informal Offer Price

Compose an email to the broker in which you explain your adjustments to the income and expenses. Explain that after applying the broker's Cap Rate, the adjusted price is X, and that you'd be happy to make an offer at the price if the seller would be amenable to that.

Send your broker something like this:

Hey Rob, I looked over the package you sent me. Everything looks good—it's what we talked about on the phone. I made a few adjustments to the underwriting, though.

Since I don't have the actual financials, I had to rely on the pro forma numbers that were included. We both know those are going to be lower than actuals, right? Well, that's all we have to work with at the moment. In your pro forma, you had vacancies at 5% of the Gross Potential Rent, which from my experience is typically closer to 10% when you include bad debt, etc.

Regarding expenses, I don't have the actuals, but the pro forma totals only add up to about 45% of income. For example, it appears the insurance expenses are missing, and not much is allotted for repairs in the P&L. Based on experience and actual financials from similar listings in the area, I know those are significantly low. I normally use 55% of income for the expenses, and that's what I'm using here.

You're advertising an 8% Cap Rate for this deal. I'm not sure if that's fair for this area, but let's assume it is. If you apply an 8% Cap Rate to the Adjusted Net Operating Income, the valuation of the building is right around $500K, quite a bit away from the $650K asking price.

If you see something awry with my underwriting, let me know. I could make an offer at asking price, but I don't want to waste your time if we both know the actual NOI will be lower than what you have in the pro forma once we get into due diligence. I'd rather be a bit more realistic upfront.

I'm not sure how flexible your seller is on the asking price, but I'd be pleased to put in an offer at $500K if he would consider it.

Let me know what you think. I look forward to hearing from you.

That's it! That's how to analyze and make an offer in 10 minutes.

Don't waste your life away analyzing deals. Work smarter, not harder. If you do, you'll be able to look at more deals and increase your chances of finding a deal that will actually work.

> If you'd like to see the 10-Minute Offer in action, then check out this three-part video course in the free Companion Course. I also cover more advanced topics, including how to create ten-year financial projections and figure out the most profitable exit strategy. To access the videos, go to FinancialFreedomTheBook.com/course > Chapter 5: Secret #3: How to Analyze Deals and Make Offers in 10 Minutes.

Learning to analyze deals is the most important skill to master early on because you won't sound like a newbie, it will increase your confidence, and you'll be able to make more offers.

A Success Story

Nick C. in New York also discovered the power of learning the skill of analyzing deals.

He had just signed up for my coaching program and a few days later went to his local REIA. He met with a potential investor who asked him about his track record, but Nick didn't have a good answer. On our next coaching call, he was pretty discouraged. I told him to be patient and finish the online training and then analyze five deals to improve his skills and confidence.

After the next REIA meeting, he got onto our coaching call with excitement. He told me that he'd met with two other potential investors during the networking break, and they *never* asked him about his track record. Within a couple of weeks, his language and confidence improved to the point he wasn't asked about his track record.

That's the power of learning the skill of analyzing deals, which in turn improves your language and increases your confidence. Once you have the confidence, people will no longer question you about your track record and Proof of Funds.

Like Nick, you are on your way to being a professional. Read on to learn the final secret to ensuring you have a never-ending supply of high-quality deals.

CHAPTER 6

Secret #4: The #1 Way to Find the Best Deals

You might be saying to yourself, "Yes, Michael, I see how analyzing deals is an important skill, but isn't it really tough to find good deals right now?"

I remember when I started flipping houses in 2005. I signed up with a local mentor who taught me how to put up bandit signs and send postcards. Not once did he say I should check the MLS for deals. Not knowing any better, I followed his advice and got my first two deals in the first three months.

It's the same thing today. Deals aren't going to fall into your lap. You know it's a numbers game with real estate, right? The more offers you make, the quicker you'll do your first deal. And now you know how to make an offer in ten minutes, so you can make many offers, quickly.

Some gurus will teach you how to market to probates, send yellow letters to apartment owners, or network with attorneys. All of these tactics can work, but I've found they can take time and can cost money.

There's a better way that will get you the best deals faster and with less work.

The #1 Way to Find Apartment Building Deals

The best and most efficient way to find great apartment building deals is *through a good network of commercial real estate (CRE) brokers.*

CRE brokers make it their business to find deals. The good ones send postcards and letters to apartment building owners and build the relationship years before an owner wants to sell. They network extensively and beat the pavement to get listings and buyers.

For years, the local Marcus & Millichap broker would call me like clockwork every three months to check in on me. They'd sometimes offer to take me out for lunch or do an informal "appraisal" of my buildings to assess what they were worth. No strings attached.

This guy's smart: he may not get a listing today, but he may get one down the road, or maybe I'll buy one of his listings.

Unfortunately, most brokers are not that good. The few good ones are worth their weight in gold, and all you need is a few of them to have a never-ending supply of good deals.

I remember when I was marketing for deals in Texas after taking my first apartment building boot camp in 2007. While I did send out letters (a lot of work, and I didn't get a single deal out of several months of marketing!), I focused heavily on cold-calling CRE brokers. Over several weeks of this, I noticed that a few brokers actually took me seriously and had deals on a regular basis. In addition, they communicated frequently, while other brokers did not. I found one broker in particular who fed me deals almost on a weekly basis.

Focus your efforts on finding just two to three brokers who are prolific deal-makers that take you seriously, and you are set for the rest of your real estate investing career.

How Do You Find Good CRE Brokers?

One of the best ways to find potential brokers to work with is on LoopNet. I hear you saying, "LoopNet is worthless for finding deals," and that is mostly true, but it's a gold mine for finding CRE brokers.

Here's the approach I use to find CRE brokers on www.LoopNet. com (it's free to create an account). I search for the kind of buildings I want to buy. I create a spreadsheet and capture the contact info of each of the CRE brokers who have listings. After doing several, I see some brokers over and over again, and I track how many listings a broker has. The more listings the better.

I then cold-call the brokers and use the script from Tip #1: Educate Yourself So You Don't Sound Like a Newbie (page 69).

If the deal in LoopNet doesn't quite match my profile, I add something like, "I saw your listing on LoopNet, and that deal doesn't really work for me, but here's what I'm looking for. What else do you have?" I may tell the broker what I'm looking for and learn a little about him or her, too. Then I see how the broker interacts with me and what his or her deal flow is.

I find an in-person meeting is a good next step if you think the broker is one of the better ones.

I track all of this activity in a spreadsheet. Over time, you'll see a few brokers bubble to the top.

3 Tips for Working with Brokers to Maintain Deal Flow

Brokers can be surprisingly difficult to work with because many of them don't respond to you and don't even send you a deal when they have one. Therefore, it's *your* responsibility to make your relationship as productive as possible.

Here are three tips I've found to be helpful in maintaining a steady deal flow from your network of brokers.

Tip #1: Be persistent. For some reason, most brokers don't respond to your first attempt at contacting them. I normally try a sequence of email, phone call, and text message to try to get that first response. If after 3–5 attempts you still don't get a response, it's time to scratch that broker off your list and move on.

Tip #2: Be responsive. What I mean by "responsive" is that when a broker sends you a deal, respond to the broker with feedback within forty-eight hours. And when I say "feedback," I mean you're making them an informal 10-Minute Offer for every deal that you get. My brokers have told me that they hear back from only about 25% of their buyers. If you're responsive, you instantly bubble up to the top of their buyer's list. Another benefit of being responsive is that the broker learns what kind of deals you like and don't like.

Tip #3: Be consistent. Stay in touch with your brokers on a regular basis. Send them an email, text, or voice mail once every 2–4 weeks so they know you're still there. Remind them of your deal criteria or send them a useful blog post or news article that might help them.

The Holy Grail of Working with Brokers: "Off-Market" Listings

You're communicating consistently and promptly with brokers, and maybe you meet them in person for lunch or to tour a property. Over time, the broker will know exactly what kind of deal you're looking for and begin to view you as a serious buyer.

When the broker is working on a new listing, he may call you up and say, "Hey, Michael, I'm working on a new listing. I think it fits the profile of what you're looking for. I won't have the listing signed yet, and the marketing package won't be ready for another ten days, but I'll send you the rent roll and financials. Take a look at it and see if you want to make an offer before it hits the market."

What just happened here?

You just got an off-market deal (also called a "pocket-listing") because the broker has not yet marketed the deal to the masses. In other words, you're not competing with the world for this one deal. This is the holy grail of broker relationships: earning your brokers' trust and becoming one of their preferred buyers so that they bring off-market opportunities to you before everyone else sees them. Getting to this takes time, so be patient. But once you get to that place (and you will!), all you need is one or two good brokers and you'll have as many deals as you can handle.

Other Ways to Find Deals

Finding deals through brokers is the best way to find deals. But if you need more deal flow and you know every broker in town, here are other ways to find deals:

:y managers. Property managers can be a great source of deals.
intimately familiar with their properties, and usually the first
to know when the owner is getting tired and wants to sell. As you
network with property managers to build your team, ask them peri-
odically if one of their owners is interested in selling. Ed Hermsen
(Podcast #48) found his first two deals that way.

Direct mail. Another way to generate leads is by sending letters
to apartment owners. You can purchase lists from list brokers like
listsource.com and have a company print and mail the letters for you
(like YellowLetters.com). The disadvantage is that direct mail costs
money and takes time, and the response rate varies. But since there
are only a limited number of apartment owners in any one city, it's
possible to send them a letter every three months on a limited budget.

Apartment Owners Association. Joining an Apartment Owners
Association is a great networking opportunity. That's where other
owners go, and it's a great way to not only find potential sellers, but
potential buyers, partners, and other professionals who can help you.

Driving for dollars. Driving for dollars can also yield results. If you
see a run-down complex, it's a sign that it's being mismanaged and
has problems. If there's a "for rent" sign, call on it and ask to speak
with the owner. They might be very glad to hear from you.

I recommend starting with commercial real estate brokers because
that will give you the fastest results. Once you know every broker in
town and need more deal flow, then consider tapping into some of
these other ways to find deals.

Apply the 4 Secrets to Getting Started with Apartment Building Investing Today

Most real estate investors considering getting started with apartment building investing struggle with one or more of these challenges:

- "I don't have any experience (and so I'll wait)."
- "I don't have the money (and so I'll wait)."
- "I don't know how to get started (and so I'll wait)."
- "I don't know how to find good deals (and so I'll wait)."

I hope you see how you can overcome each of these challenges by:

- educating yourself, using scripts, and building your team so that you appear more experienced than you really are and don't sound like a newbie.;
- raising money from others;
- getting started by learning how to analyze deals and make 10-Minute Offers with confidence; and
- building relationships with brokers who will feed you all the deals you need.

Now that you know the four secrets to overcoming each of these challenges, you can start your journey toward financial freedom with apartments *today*!

No more excuses.

You have all the tools you need to succeed. Next, I'm going to give you a clear plan of action, so you'll know exactly what to do to close your first deal in the next twelve months (or sooner). And once you do, the Law of the First Deal will put you on a path to retirement in three to five years.

PART III

The Financial Freedom Blueprint: 7 Steps to Quitting Your Job in 3–5 Years

CHAPTER 7

Step #1: Determine (and Reduce!) Your Rat Race Number

Remember the "ONE thing" for becoming financially free with real estate?

That's right ... it's your first deal.

Because the Law of the First Deal states that if you do your first multifamily deal (of any size), you will become financially free in three to five years. But you'll never get there if you don't know how to take the steps to get to that first deal. That's why I developed the Financial Freedom Blueprint, the most comprehensive and unique system for showing you step-by-step how to become (permanently) financially free with real estate in the next three to five years.

The 7-step Financial Freedom Blueprint takes you on a journey from properly setting your goals, to getting started, to closing your first deal, to becoming financially free. The step-by-step roadmap I'm about to share with you is what has worked for me and hundreds of others who have come before you, and it will work for you. Let's get started with the first step:

Step #1: Determine (and Reduce!) Your Rat Race Number

In his book *Rich Dad Poor Dad*, Robert Kiyosaki defines financial freedom as the point at which you can cover your living expenses with passive income. I call this the "Rat Race Number." Once you've achieved that, you are financially free and can do whatever you want—like quit your job, travel more, spend time with family, pursue non-profit aspirations, etc.

There are two ways to achieve your Rat Race Number:

Increase your passive income, and

Decrease your expenses.

Let's first figure out how to calculate your Rat Race Number so that we can be clear about our goals.

The process of determining your Rat Race Number is to figure out what you're CURRENTLY spending and what you could do to decrease those expenses.

How Much Are You Currently Spending?

If you're not tracking your spending, then start doing it right now. It's at the core of sound personal financial management. I've been doing this every single month for many years.

A great tool to use is Mint.com. It's an online tool and mobile app that makes it extremely easy to track your spending and prevent you from exceeding your budget. You can also create a spreadsheet to track your expenses.

In order to establish your average monthly spending, I suggest tracking three months of expenses.

How Can You Spend Less?

Next, look at each expense category and figure out what you could do without.

This is a really painful step, I know.

We love the way our life is! We're used to the French vanilla caramel macchiato each day. We love our 1,800+ cable channels. We love our brand-new cars and houses. I get it. I love 'em, too.

But think about this: How badly do you want to be financially free? If you really want that, then could you do without some of the things you've grown accustomed to?

If you need help with this, I highly recommend Dave Ramsey's Financial Peace University. This course helps you determine your expenses, create a budget, pay off your debt, and save for the future. You can complete an online course or join a group near you, and it's very affordable.

Think about it this way: A reasonable rental property should put at least $100 per month in your pocket after all expenses. So for every $100 you save per month, it's about the same as purchasing one rental property. If you could shave $1,000 off per month, it's like doing your first 10-unit apartment building!

So don't skip this step. Really ask yourself what expenses you can do without and what changes you could make (and tolerate!) to save money. The lower your Rat Race Number, the faster you'll become financially free.

I'm not just telling you to do something without knowing what it's like.

I've been through this myself, from tweaking my spending to actually downsizing my house. It was one of the hardest things I've ever had to do.

We had our dream home, a six-bedroom house on nearly an acre in one of the nicest areas in Northern Virginia. I had a good job at my software company and was flush with money from the IPO.

But after I decided to quit and become a full-time entrepreneur, we struggled financially for a number of years, and I felt like we needed to downsize to make ends meet. My wife wasn't on board because she loved that house. After some time, she agreed that for me to continue working from home, we should sell the house. We decided to move farther into the suburbs, which would substantially reduce our housing costs.

That also meant we had to tell our friends, many of whom didn't understand why we were doing what we were doing. We had to tell the kids that they could no longer play with their neighborhood friends.

It was a pretty dark time for the family.

But I can tell you that this move was blessed. We connected with an even better community of friends, both for us and the kids. We cut our housing costs nearly in half (it was like buying ten rental houses!), and it allowed me to continue working from home so I could attend my kids' events during the day.

Looking back on that time, I'm not sure what would have happened if we hadn't had the courage to downsize. I think the expenses would have forced me to go back and get a job, and that's not what we wanted. I wanted to be financially free—not for a year or two, but permanently. My high living expenses were making that nearly impossible.

So I highly encourage you to sit down with your spouse and examine your living expenses.

What are you prepared to do to reach your goals?

What's Your Rat Race Number?

Let's assume you recorded your ACTUAL spending and made some changes to reduce your monthly expenses by 20% each month.

And let's say you determined that you could live with $5,000 per month if you really tightened your belt. That's $60,000 per year.

You might be thinking, *Yes, Michael, but what about taxes?*

The nice thing about investing in real estate is that you'll likely be paying substantially less taxes (possibly none at all) on your apartment building income. That's because the IRS allows you to depreciate the value of the building. This depreciation is counted as an expense on your tax return (which reduces your taxable income) even though it's not an actual expense that affects your cash flow.

Taxation of real estate is beyond the scope of this book, but suffice it to say that your taxes on real estate income are substantially less than with your W-2 income, and chances are, you might not be paying any taxes on that income. Check with your tax advisor.

Okay, I hope you get my point about real estate taxes. For the purpose of this exercise, let's assume that you need to cover $5,000 in living expenses.

How Will You Get There?

For many of you, this may be the first time you're doing this exercise. It's eye-opening, huh?

Once you have your Rat Race Number, the next question is: How will you get there?

You now know that you need $5,000 in passive income each month.

What real estate strategy will get you there the quickest?

If you're flipping houses right now, then you know that there's hardly anything *passive* about that (I flipped over thirty houses, so I know a little bit about this!). So flipping houses is NOT going to be the kind of activity that generates passive income.

What about building a rental portfolio? This certainly qualifies as a passive income activity, so put a check mark there.

How many houses would you need to get to $5,000 in monthly income? This depends on your market and how good of an investor you are. Let's say you're consistently able to get $200 per month in cash flow (after expenses, including vacancies and repairs!) from your rental houses.

That's great!

But at $200 per month in passive income, you would need twenty-five houses to retire. That's a lot of houses. Do you have the capital for that? How long would it take for you to build such a portfolio? Do you even want that many houses? Have you ever thought about this?

Don't Skip this Step!

You might be tempted to skirt around this step because it is painful and potentially life altering. But Step #1 of the Financial Freedom Blueprint is critical because it can accelerate your financial goals, often substantially. As you might know from playing the CASHFLOW 101 game, getting out of the rat race as a high-income earner (like an attorney) is much more difficult than if you're a janitor. Even though the attorney has a higher income, his expenses are also much higher, and it takes longer to cover those expenses with passive income.

It would have taken me a LOT longer to become financially free had I not downsized my house and started living on a budget.

So don't skip this step in your quest for financial freedom. As I said before, every $100 you save is like buying one rental property.

If you determined that you needed one hundred units to replace your $10,000 monthly income and were able to reduce your living expenses by $2,000, then it's as if you just bought twenty units. It's the "easiest" first deal you can do because you have the most control over it. And suddenly you're 20% toward achieving your financial goal.

So go enroll in Dave Ramsey's Financial Peace University right now!

Reducing your living expenses *and* building your passive income with apartments is a powerful combination.

Now that we've covered this very important first step of the Financial Freedom Blueprint, we can proceed with the next step, which is to complete your "Vision Map" so that you know where you're going and how to get there.

CHAPTER 8

Step #2: Complete Your Vision Map

In this step, I want you to become really clear about your goals and develop a path to achieve those goals. While you should have goals for different parts of your life (relationships, spirituality, health, etc.), for the purpose of this exercise, I'm referring to goals related to achieving financial freedom with real estate.

The problem is that most people don't believe they can become financially free with real estate because the mere thought of it seems overwhelming.

We all want to be successful real estate investors so that we can retire and do the things we REALLY want to do. And in order to be successful, we're taught to think big. Only if we think big can we really achieve greatness. That's because if we don't think big, we're limited by our own experience, skills, and comfort zone. Thinking big forces us to think outside the box and outside of our comfort zone. It makes us think not of what's probable, but what is possible.

The problem with thinking big comes when it's divorced from actionable goals that pave the way to reaching those big dreams. In other words, you need to think BIG but have a small-scale PLAN, at least enough of one to know what you should be doing next.

To connect the dream with the plan, I have my students go through a process I call the "Vision Map Exercise". I call it by that name because it combines "Vision" (i.e., thinking big) with a map (or plan) of how to get there. The map consists of milestones over twelve months, ninety days, and this week.

How the Vision Map Works

You can create a Vision Map for every area of your life: business/ financial, health, relationships, recreation (fun!), spirituality, giving, and any other area that's important to you. For each area of your life, write down an "I am" statement for what you want to be, do, or have. I encourage you to write these in the present tense, which helps you to visualize yourself reaching this goal.

For example, let's assume you have a financial dream of quitting your job in three to five years by accumulating multifamily units. You might have this "I am" statement:

I am financially free. I no longer have to work for money.

This is your BIG idea, your vision.

Next, you associate a goal with the big idea so that you know if you've achieved it. This goal is specific, measurable, and written in the present tense, like this:

By (such and such date), I am earning $10,000 per month in passive income.

If you're starting from zero, then you might have no idea of how you're going to accomplish this goal. That's a GREAT sign of thinking BIG. So far so good.

Next, you want to break this down into a twelve-month goal, perhaps something like this:

I have closed on my first deal (10–20 units), and it cash flows $2,500 per month.

This starts to become a bit more real! Instead of a daunting goal of $10K per month, you just have to focus on that ONE thing: the first deal, a 10- to 20-unit apartment building.

Next, translate that twelve-month goal into a ninety-day goal. I like the ninety-day time frame because it's long enough to achieve something meaningful but short enough to see yourself achieving the goal if you hustle. Something like this:

In ninety days, I have built my team of property managers and lenders, met with ten investors, analyzed fifty deals, and made twenty offers.

Definitely an achievable goal if you work at it. And, finally, translate that into your goals for THIS week, perhaps like this:

This week I have spoken with one property manager, met with one potential investor, and analyzed five deals.

And now what you need to do TODAY becomes much clearer:

Today I will call one property manager.

It's critical that you think BIG, no question. But many people fail to connect their big thinking with what they need to do TODAY, right now. And if you can't do that, you'll feel overwhelmed and give up before you even get started. So don't fall into the "think big" trap.

plete the Vision Map exercise to gain clarity not only about your
٫ ᴏn but about how to get there.

You can download a Vision Map template from the Companion
Course. It contains the steps of the Financial Freedom
Blueprint. Start with those and modify them to meet your
personal goals and vision.

To download the Vision Map template, go to
FinancialFreedomTheBook.com/course > Chapter 8: Complete
Your Vision Map > Lesson #1: Vision Map and 90-Day Plan.

Now that we're clear about what we want (and don't want), it's time
to move on to the next step in the Financial Freedom Blueprint: The
Pre-Launch Sequence.

CHAPTER 9

Step #3: The Pre-Launch Sequence (The First 30 Days)

The Pre-Launch Sequence is about developing the minimal skill set and confidence to be released into the world without sounding like a newbie. I'm going to show you how to become a "seasoned" multifamily investor in just thirty days. Here is the week-by-week plan:

Week 1: Educate Yourself So You Don't Sound Like a Newbie

In the first week, you're going to educate yourself. The problem is that most people don't even know where to get started with apartment building investing or raising money. They lack the knowledge to do certain things, or they don't have the scripts and tools to get them started.

The solution, of course, is a good system, one that teaches you how to evaluate deals and raise money—that's a must. I have a system called The Ultimate Guide to Buying Apartment Buildings with Private Money, but it doesn't have to be my system—there are others out there.

My main point is to do it so you learn the language, key investing concepts, and the tactical steps to get your first deal done. Don't get stuck with classroom learning—knock it out in the first week, and then quickly move to week 2.

Now that you've completed your "basic training," it's critical to become crystal clear about your first deal. And that's what we're going to do next.

Week 2: Clarify Your First Deal

This week I want you to get really clear about your first deal. The problem is that most people skip this step and chase after deals without a clear picture of what that first deal looks like. As a result, they either do a deal that's too small or they pursue a deal that is too big and then fail to do a deal at all.

If we clearly define our first deal, it will allow us to visualize what that first deal will look like. If we can visualize it, the more real it becomes; and the more real it becomes, the more likely we will be to achieve that critical goal along our path to financial freedom.

Clarity of your first deal is key.

Your first deal should be both meaningful **and** achievable. *Meaningful* in that it should allow you to make measurable progress toward your goal of financial freedom. Typically that means it should be as big as possible. *Achievable*, meaning that, while your deal should be as big as possible, it should also be achievable in the next twelve months.

Everyone's first deal is going to be a bit different. It requires an honest review of your goals and personal financial situation.

If your Rat Race Number is $10,000 per month then there's a

higher chance that you have some savings to invest with, and you are more likely to know other people with money to invest. Therefore, a reasonable first deal might be a 20-unit apartment building since it's feasible for you to raise $250,000 in the next three to six months.

On the other hand, if your Rat Race Number is $4,000, you might have very limited savings and be less likely to know other high net worth individuals. If that's your situation, then a reasonable first deal might be a duplex or 4-plex.

If you pick a first deal that is not *achievable*, you're likely going to give up. If you pick a first deal that is not *meaningful*, it might take you longer than three to five years to become financially free. Remember this: the "best" first deal is one that is both meaningful and achievable in the next twelve months.

Where to Invest?

In addition to the size of the first deal, the second most important question to answer is where that first deal should be.

In general, we're looking for an area that is growing and can achieve a reasonable return.

This disqualifies areas such as San Francisco or New York City, because even though these areas are growing economically, yields are so low that it makes it difficult for the average entrepreneur to achieve a reasonable return for the investors.

What if you live in one of these areas?

The solution is to look outside of your area.

It's not that hard.

These days, geography should NOT be a factor or excuse. So much is available online that you complete the work virtually, and if you must visit in person, you can reach nearly every US destination with a five-hour flight. The only reason you would *not* go outside your own area is because you want to stay in your comfort zone. And do we grow in our comfort zone? I think you know the answer.

The next question, then, becomes: How do you find the *right* area in which to invest?

How to Choose the Best Areas for Multifamily Deals with Confidence

One of the main challenges when getting started with multifamily investing is where to look. With the market so hot, many investors are looking outside their own backyards in search of deals.

But where to look? How do you go about it?

This is not a small matter because wherever you choose means that's where you'll spend hours and days looking for deals, building teams, and managing the property.

The methodology is to evaluate areas based on the following criteria:

- **Look for areas you like.** Start by picking an area you like (or at least wouldn't mind spending time in). Maybe you have friends and family who live there, or maybe it's just an area you like. Also consider the travel logistics. Is it a place you can reasonably drive or fly to? For example, I like to be able to get to the location with a direct flight in two hours or less.

- **Look for "high-yield" areas.** If you're living on either coast (or

116

even some areas in between), then you know that the multifamily market is red-hot. It will be more difficult to find good deals when others are willing to overpay. That means you may have to look in less-hot cities or secondary markets that may be off the beaten path but offer higher yields. "High-yield" areas are properties that are valued for less relative to their income than other areas (i.e., their cash-on-cash returns are higher, as well as their Cap Rates).

- **Look for "high-growth" areas.** You want areas in which employment is growing and ideally, you want that source of employment to be as diversified as possible. This will help avoid what happened during the recession with areas that relied on only a few industries.

I want to be more specific about how to apply these criteria by using three very useful reports.

3 Reports to Help You Find the Right Area

Here are three free reports to help you evaluate markets in which to invest.

The Marcus & Millichap National Apartment Report. To access this report, visit their website and create a free account. The report ranks the top metropolitan areas in the country by these very important criteria:

- Vacancy and rent rates trends
- Sales trends
- Cap Rate and yield
- Employment growth

The IRR Viewpoint Report. Another useful report is the IRR Viewpoint report, available on the IRR website. This report plots major cities on the "Market Cycle" graph (i.e., from a "Recovery/ Expansion" market to "Hyper Supply" and back down to "Recession"). And it does this for multiple asset classes (i.e., multifamily, retail, office, etc.) and for major cities across the country.

The report visually plots the major markets on where they are in the "up-and-down" market cycle. It's interesting that there are a couple of markets that are still in "recovery." Surprisingly, there are also a good number of markets in growth and not-yet-hot markets (i.e., "expanding").

Ideally, you want to look for markets that are in the Recovery and Expansion cycles and avoid properties in the Hyper-Supply and Recession cycles.

The Milken Best Performing Cities Report. The third useful report is the Milken Best Performing Cities Report, which you can download from Milken Institute. This report ranks cities—200 large and 200 small cities—based on their job growth and highlights the top-ranked cities with a more in-depth profile.

This allows you to see where your city ranks in the list and how it's trending. If your city is toward the lower end of the list and declining, it could be an indication to be cautious about investing in that city. On the other hand, if your city is growing and the trend is positive, that might be a good indication to invest there.

Where to Start: Putting It All Together

This is a lot of information, and you might be completely over-whelmed by the thought of picking one area from many.

Why not start with the IRR Viewpoint report? Create a short list from the cities in the Recovery or Expansion Market Cycle. Then check out the High-Yield Markets in the Marcus & Millichap report and cross reference them with the Markets with the Highest Expected Employment Growth. Combine these with the places you wouldn't mind spending time, and you might have three to five cities on your short list. Then use the rest of the reports to drill down on each of these cities further and pick your top three.

These three reports will help you identify markets in which to look for deals. If you can couple solid job growth with an Expanding Market cycle and high Cap Rates, you have an ideal combination to look in that market. However, keep in mind that real estate investing is still very local; just because a city has a low ranking in the Best Cities report doesn't mean that one part of the city isn't growing. And vice versa. So take these statistics with a grain of salt.

Nevertheless, this methodology in combination with these three reports is a useful tool for narrowing down a geographic location for your next multifamily deal.

Week 3: Analyze 5 Deals to Gain Confidence

This week we want to get a jump start on developing the skill to quickly and accurately analyze deals. Once you analyze at least five deals, you no longer sound like a newbie, you're able to make offers more quickly and accurately, and your confidence level increases tantially. If you can do that, brokers will return your phone calls and investors will agree to meet with you.

We already covered how to analyze deals in Secret #3: How to Analyze Deals and Make Offers in 10 Minutes (page 83), so go back to that section if you need a refresher.

In order to analyze a deal, you'll need a good financial model to help you. You can build your own spreadsheet, search for one on the Internet, or purchase my Syndicated Deal Analyzer.

Find the best one for you, just make sure:

- It's created for analyzing multifamily property;
- It includes purchase and exit assumptions;
- It has the ability to create ten-year financial projections;
- It incorporates investor returns; and
- The software is editable so that you can customize the model.

Once you have a good financial model, it's time to get to work. Here are some ways to get deals to analyze:

- **LoopNet:** Go on loopnet.com, create a free account, and search for multifamily properties. There will *not* be a shortage of properties on LoopNet! You may need to contact the broker to get the financials.

- **MLS:** You can also go to www.realtor.com (where houses are listed) and find multifamily listings.

- **Log into the Companion Course:** You can access five sample deals there. Ignore my video analysis for the moment and instead just download the marketing package. Once you've analyzed it yourself, you can compare it to my analysis.

Go to FinancialFreedomTheBook.com/course > Chapter 9: The Pre-Launch Sequence.

Quantity over Quality!

For this step, it is **NOT** important how good the deal is, or even if it matches your first deal criteria. Find a deal, any deal, and analyze it. Do this five times.

If you're calling brokers and they won't call you back or send you their marketing package, then find another deal or download one from the Companion Course. This step is NOT about calling brokers, it's about analyzing deals.

Okay?

Okay ... let's move on to next week.

Week 4: Complete the Sample Deal Package to Raise Money

Find a deal you already analyzed in Week 3 that matches your criteria for your first deal from Week 2 and create a Sample Deal Package from that.

We already covered How to Create the Sample Deal Package (page 50) under Secret #1: Raise All of the Money You Need to Do Your First Deal (page 43), so refer to that chapter for a refresher and instructions for how to download a template.

Not only is the Sample Deal Package a critical tool to help you raise money, it also helps you visualize that first deal. Visualization is used by top athletes and is taught by prestigious coaches like Tony Robbins and many others. Why? Because it works.

The more you can visualize something, the more real it becomes. And the more real it becomes, the more you believe. And the more you believe, the faster it becomes reality.

Congratulations! You've completed the first thirty days of the Pre-Launch Sequence. You've educated yourself so that you don't sound like a newbie, you've clarified your first deal, increased your skills and confidence by learning to analyze deals, and created the Sample Deal Package to raise money.

You are now ready to be released into the world as an apartment building entrepreneur!

Time to launch!

CHAPTER 10

Step #4: Launch (The Next 60 Days)

In the Pre-Launch Sequence, you developed your critical skills and increased your confidence level so that you're ready to contact brokers and investors without sounding like a newbie.

The Launch Step is more about action and less about outcome. What's most important in this step is *consistent activity to create new habits*. Here are the three activities you should be doing each week:

- **Activity #1:** Analyze and make offers
- **Activity #2:** Meet with potential investors
- **Activity #3:** Build your A-Team

Let's examine each activity in more detail:

Activity #1: Analyze and Make Offers

In order to continue building confidence and create a deal pipeline, you'll need to find and analyze deals. You might set a goal to do five deals per week, which is one per day. Adjust this number based on your available time. The more the better because, like any kind of real estate investing, this is a numbers game.

When I say analyze five deals, that includes making an informal

10-Minute Offer for each deal you analyze. This means you're getting back to the broker with something like, "The asking price won't work for me, and here's why, and here's the price that would work—is there any flexibility?"

In order for you to consistently complete this step each week, you're going to have to call brokers. We already covered this step in Secret #4: The #1 Way to Find the Best Deals (page 91), so review that section if you need to.

Remember that consistency and persistence are key.

Activity #2: Meet with Potential Investors

In addition to analyzing deals to build a deal pipeline, you also want to build a pipeline of investors. If you can get verbal commitments from investors *before* you get a deal under contract, you can make offers with confidence.

We already outlined the process of finding and connecting with potential investors in Secret #1: Raise All of the Money You Need to Do Your First Deal (page 43). Now classroom time is over; it's time to actually do it!

A reasonable goal is to meet with one potential investor per week. In order to have one meeting per week with a potential investor, you'll need to create your mind map and contact ten potential investors each week to schedule one meeting. Just like with the previous activity, consistency is key. Always contact and speak with potential investors. Once the relationship is ready, ask them for a meeting to discuss potentially investing with you.

Don't be too concerned about outcome. Talk and meet with anyone who will give you the time of day—even if you know they have no money. It's about practicing and building confidence.

Just do it.

Activity #3: Build Your A-Team

Long before you have your first deal under contract, you should have identified these other members of your team:

- Property manager
- Landlord/tenant attorney
- Real estate attorney
- SEC attorney
- Commercial lenders and brokers
- Property inspector
- Appraiser
- Insurance agent

Your success as an apartment building investor depends on the strength of your team. So don't cut corners, and build the best team you can.

The best way to find your team members is through *referrals*. Yes, you can search on the Internet and go to the proper association website, but I like referrals better than any other method. In fact, you don't just want a referral to someone based on his or her reputation, you prefer referrals to people that your contacts have actually done business with, so they can personally vouch for them.

One of the best ways to get referrals is through your commercial real estate brokers. Ask them for professionals they really like and with whom they've done business.

In general, ask EVERYONE you speak to for a referral. If you're speaking to a broker, ask for a referral to a property manager. If you're speaking to a property manager, ask for a referral to an insurance agent, and so on.

I recommend that you track your activity in a spreadsheet using these columns:

- Name and contact info
- Type of team member (i.e., property manager, mortgage broker, etc.) so that you can quickly sort by team member type
- Who referred you to that person
- Activity Log: date with narrative of the conversation and/or email

The Most Important Member of Your Team to Recruit as Soon as Possible

The property manager is by far the most important member of your team to recruit long before you have your first deal under contract. He or she can help you during the due diligence phase with things like rental comps, vacancy rates, and inspections.

Avoid this situation at all costs: you find a nice 21-unit with good upside, get a Letter of Intent signed, and even succeed in getting some money raised. Then it occurs to you that maybe you should have a coach or mentor review the deal with you, and he asks you questions like, "How do you know that the rents are $100 under market?" or "Why do you think you can charge back the utilities to the tenants?"

You tell him that you checked the rents on rentometer.com and they were $100 higher than the current rents. Oh, and you weren't sure about the second question.

Doing an armchair rental analysis, even if you're using an excellent tool like rentometer.com, is not enough at this stage in the game. You either need to do your own rental analysis—by calling or visiting competing apartment complexes—or, better yet, you need to be able to rely on a good local property manager who can confirm your assumptions.

If you don't have a property manager on board who's willing to help you at this stage, you're flying blind—especially if you're investing in an area you're not familiar with. The solution is to find at least one property manager long before you put a property under contract, someone you can call on if you get close to getting a deal.

They can help you at this stage by driving by the property to give you feedback about what they see. They can advise you about rents, common practices (like charging back rents), and rule of thumb for expenses. Later, during due diligence, they continue being an asset by inspecting the property with you, estimating repair costs, and coming up with pro forma financials.

Do not skip this step! That way, you'll be able to hit the ground running as you get close to getting a deal under contract!

The Second Most Important Team Member

The second most important member to have on your team before you put a property under contract is one or more commercial real estate mortgage brokers. Before you put an apartment building deal under contract, you should clearly understand your potential lenders' loan terms and underwriting criteria.

Imagine this: You put a deal under contract, and you assume a down payment of 20%, and you later find that you'll need to put 30% down. Or that you don't personally qualify for the loan and you'll need to find a co-sponsor. Or that the lender requires a six-month reserve that you didn't count on.

While sometimes ignorance is bliss, in this case these surprises could cost you a deal.

The lesson learned is this: clearly understand the terms of the potential loan and how the lender will underwrite the deal. To *underwrite* is a fancy term that refers to how the lender assesses the risk of the project, what they require of you as the sponsor to mitigate those risks, how it satisfies their lending guidelines, and the ultimate terms of the loan.

In order to understand your lender's underwriting criteria, make sure you network with potential mortgage brokers or lenders long *before* you start making offers on deals.

At this point in the teaching, I typically get at least one of three questions:

- **How many deals do I need to look at to get one?** As I said before, deals aren't just going to fall into your lap. Many people think that if they make a few offers they will get a deal. Experience just doesn't validate this. I see more like a 100 to 10 to 1 ratio: for every 100 deals you analyze, you'll submit an LOI for 10, and end up closing 1 deal. This means that if you're analyzing two deals per week, it would take you about a year to get one deal. If you want to do your first deal as quickly as possible, map out the number of deals you need to analyze each week and then execute!

- **How much time do I need to commit to be successful?** Let me start by saying everyone I know who became a full-time investor got started when they had a full-time job. Practically speaking, if you can carve out ten hours per week, you will be successful. That might be an hour in the morning or evening to analyze deals and make offers, and another hour during the day to make phone calls. We find time for things that we want or like. If you're not making the time, then you don't want financial freedom. There's nothing wrong with that, just ask yourself what you want, and you will find how you're spending your time.

- **How do I continue to take action?** Is it possible that you're not on track because you're too busy? You don't know where to start? You're overwhelmed by the whole idea? Then may I suggest you start by taking TINY action. Not MASSIVE action. While this is widely taught, it only works for something like 9% of the population. TINY action is doing TINY things each and every day until they produce MASSIVE results in the future. Could you carve out an extra thirty minutes per day to dedicate to real estate? Could you buy a notebook and write down the three things you should do next and then do them? I guarantee if you do these two TINY things each day for the next thirty days, YOU WILL BE AMAZED AT HOW FAR YOU'VE COME. Let me tell you a story to illustrate what this might look like.

Sam and Frank

Sam and Frank dream of financial freedom through real estate. They're both about the same age and have a similar house, families, time, and economic resources.

One evening they attend their first real estate club meeting. They quickly become convinced that investing in apartment buildings by raising money is the way to achieve their financial goals and quit their jobs in three to five years. After twelve months, neither of them has a deal or any money raised. On the surface, it looks like neither of them has made any progress whatsoever.

So it seems remarkable when, six months later, Sam does his first deal: a small 15-unit building about a three-hour drive from his house. He was barely able to raise the $100,000 he needed to buy the building, and it looked a bit dicey a week or so before closing because one of his investors pulled out at the last minute.

But nine months after that, Sam closed on a 56-unit deal, which required $750,000 in investor capital to close.

An overnight success.

Frank still has a good job he doesn't like very much, but he's comfortable. He attended several more boot camps and even signed up with a coach. But after eighteen months, he still hasn't done his first deal or raised any money.

Why?

Because he never took action. And I'm not talking about MASSIVE action. I'm talking about TINY action.

Here's what I mean:

After attending the real estate club meeting, Sam decided that he needed to make time for his real estate investment goals. He decided that he would watch thirty minutes less TV before he went to bed and listen to a real estate podcast or read a book on the subject instead.

Frank did not make a change to his leisure time.

After another month, Sam watched another thirty minutes less TV, and after another month, he found he had no interest in watching TV at all. Instead, he was voraciously consuming all he could about real estate.

Sam was offered a promotion at work and was thrilled. But he thought about it and decided that the extra responsibility would give him less time to learn about real estate, so he declined.

Frank, too, was offered a promotion and is now head of his department. But he works ten hours a day, takes work home, and travels two to three times a month.

Sam bought a notebook and wrote down the next three things he needed to do. They were normally simple things, like "Read 10 pages of this book," "Call a friend and tell him about my real estate investing," or "Attend the real estate club meeting this week."

Small things. Easy things. Things that ANYONE could do without trying very hard or making any big sacrifices.

Just three things.

And then he would cross them off and add three new ones.

After six long months of doing this every day, Sam looked up and was surprised at the progress he had made: brokers were sending him deals, he had spoken with about a dozen potential investors, he had analyzed close to twenty-five deals, and made a dozen offers. But he was frustrated that he didn't have a deal and hadn't raised any money yet.

Frank wasn't any better off. He didn't have a deal, either.

But he also wasn't tracking his next three to-dos in a notebook. The whole thing overwhelmed him, and he didn't know where to start.

What About You?

Are you like Sam or perhaps a little more like Frank?

How are you doing with your goals for this year?

Conclusion

The Launch Step is all about consistent activity to build the habits of analyzing deals (and making offers), meeting with potential investors, and building your team. It's not about outcome. It's quantity over quality.

This means that you might be analyzing a deal you know won't work. That's okay. Analyze it and make an offer anyway.

You might be meeting with a friend who you know doesn't have any money to invest. That's okay. Use it as an opportunity to practice.

If you tend toward analysis/paralysis, then it's time to stop reading another book or attending another seminar, and it's time to take action. If you're a perfectionist, then this step might be a challenge for you because you're trying to have all your ducks in a row before you call the first broker. You might want your website done and your business cards ordered before you schedule your first investor meeting.

You don't need perfection; you need action. Don't overthink it; just do it.

Take TINY action each and every day.

CHAPTER 11

Step #5: Build Your Pipeline

I told you that the Launch Step is all about activity and not so much about outcome. However, if you do the work, you will invariably get an outcome without even trying: you will have a pipeline of deals and investors, and have your team on the ground ready to go.

The "Pipeline Step" is all about continuing to make offers and raising money to build your pipeline. And the bigger your pipeline, the faster you'll do your first deal.

In addition to making offers, you'll also have to deal with mental challenges to survive what I call "the graveyard of apartment building investing."

Keys to Surviving the "Graveyard" of Apartment Building Investing

After a few months, the excitement begins to wane, and the entrepreneur becomes frustrated by the apparent lack of progress. As a result, many give up their quest for financial freedom for two primary reasons:

- #1: Lack of support and community
- #2: Delays, setbacks, and challenges

Working with hundreds of students, I've found that these feelings of despair affect *every* entrepreneur at one time or another—sometimes more than once. The key is how you respond to them. Let's drill down on each of these so that you're in the best position to handle and overcome them.

Reason #1: Lack of Support and Community

Being a real estate entrepreneur seeking your first apartment building deal is a lonely sport. Chances are you don't have a single friend or family member who has done what you want to do. In fact, many of or your friends and family members think you're crazy and are doing nothing to encourage you on your journey.

Then there's the issue of who to turn to when you have a question.

Even the best course or seminar won't be able to address every possible situation you might encounter, because every deal is different. Who can you turn to when you have a question? Are you buying right? Are you too eager to do a deal? What should you do about the mold issue you uncovered during due diligence?

Many of these questions can paralyze you if you don't have someone to turn to for support.

The key to succeeding in this step is to get some kind of support and join a community of like-minded entrepreneurs.

My wife's been doing this "Insanity Max: 30" DVD workout program in which you try to hang with drill sergeant Shaun T until you have to take a break, at which point you've "maxed out."

Truly insane.

I play tennis competitively, therefore, I'm in pretty good shape. Or so I thought until I did one of these sessions. Sheesh.

I maxed out at minute 10 and never really recovered. My wife was egging me on, at first encouraging me and then calling me a baby, which worked for a little while until I finally gave up at around minute 20.

Then it dawned on me.

If I really wanted to get in shape, I should exercise more and maybe even do this Insanity Max program. The problem is that I don't love exercising, so completing the program is a major challenge for me. What would really help me is for someone to hold me accountable and be supportive.

It's the same thing for most new real estate investors: a lack of support and community is one of the major reasons they quit.

But not to worry! Here are three tips to help you overcome this challenge.

Tip #1: Find an accountability partner. It's a proven fact that for every one hundred people who attend a seminar, only ten will actually take action. If you're one of the 90% of people who *don't* naturally stick with something after they start it, you will need an accountability partner, someone who will encourage you and keep you accountable. This person could be a spouse, friend, or someone you pay (like a coach or mentor).

It doesn't matter so much which one of those you seek out, but you *must* align yourself with a person like that. Otherwise, your efforts will peter out sooner or later.

So make sure you have an accountability partner.

Tip #2: Surround yourself with like-minded people. For the exercise session, my accountability partner was my wife, who encouraged me to join her and reminded me of my goal to get into better shape. But as much as she tried, she failed to get me through the entire thirty minutes. She was only my wife, and if I embarrassed myself in front of her, well, it wasn't a big deal—I do this all the time. *Wink wink.*

But what if there were six other people in the room? Surely, I would have tried harder!

The same is true of your real estate start-up business. Make sure you surround yourself with a community of like-minded entrepreneurs who are working toward the same goals and can support you.

On good days, you want to share your successes. But who can truly understand and appreciate what you've accomplished? And on bad days, you need someone to tell you that it will be okay, that it's all worthwhile, just keep going. Who really understands what we go through?

Right, very few people, especially our friends and family.

That's why you need to seek out a community of like-minded entrepreneurs.

Again, it doesn't matter as much what *kind* of community you have, but it *does* matter that you're a part of one. The community could be a mastermind group. Maybe you create one from the people you meet at the boot camp, or perhaps you pay to join one. In-person is best, but a virtual or online community is an excellent (and often more practical) alternative.

Either way, unpaid or paid, in-person or virtual, you *must* be part of a community. This will ensure the longevity of your actions and the eventual success of your venture.

Tip #3: Find a mentor. Top athletes have coaches. Top actors have coaches. Even the most successful businesspeople have coaches.

Do you have a coach?

If not, you're going to struggle to achieve your goals. It'll take longer, and you'll make a lot more mistakes than necessary. You're going to encounter situations you've never seen, and a mentor can help you navigate those unchartered waters. You can recruit a mentor who agrees to meet you for lunch every so often and answer your questions. You may be able to find more experienced apartment building investors like that at your local REIA or by asking around.

I recommend that you build an "advisory board" of more experienced investors—they are invaluable. However, I've found that most of the time you're not going to get the kind of support you need from "volunteer" mentors, especially in the beginning. That's why I think it's best to hire a coach who can help you do your first deal. Not every successful real estate entrepreneur has a paid coach, but they have all had a mentor or advisor.

One of the two main reasons people quit their pursuit of the first apartment building deal is because they did not address the issue of support. The solution is to find an accountability partner, start or join a community of like-minded people, and find an experienced mentor or coach. If you follow these tips, your chances for success skyrocket.

Reason #2: Delays, Setbacks, and Challenges

Right around three months after people decide to get started with apartment building investing, the initial adrenaline wears off and they become frustrated that they haven't done a deal or raised any money yet. And, frankly, it's more work than they thought it would be. They might say to themselves, "I don't think this multifamily thing works. Or maybe it works for others, but not for me."

Here are some tips for dealing with these days of doubt and discouragement.

Tip #1: Revisit your why. Remember the Vision Map Exercise (page 109)? Now it's time to revisit your Vision Map and review *why* you decided to embark on this crazy journey in the first place. Was it to quit your job? To escape the constant pressure of having to provide for your family? Why was that important? So that you could regain control of your time to do whatever you wanted, whenever you wanted, and with whom you wanted? And why was that important? Was it perhaps to spend more time with your growing children? To improve the relationship with your spouse? To travel more?

Whatever it was for you, go back to the time when you decided to get started with multifamily investing. What pain were you running from? What better things did you want for yourself and your family?

If this tip doesn't keep you going, then redo the Vision Map Exercise. But this time *really* do it. Spend time on it. Meditate over it. Involve your spouse and family.

One of my favorite quotes is from Tony Robbins: "It is in your moments of decision that your destiny is shaped."[4]

I find that whenever a person truly *decides* something, the only possible outcome is *action*. Whenever I see a person *not* taking action, and I probe further, I find that the person has not truly *decided*. They may say they want something, but they're lying to themselves and others.

This is why it's important that you *decide*, right now, if you want to change your life or you want to have the same life you have right now this time next year. If you do, that's fine too, but if you don't, then *decide* right now that you want a different life. Once you do, you will find that you're naturally taking action. The universe will give you what you truly want. I've seen it in my own life and in many others, too. But you have to *decide*.

Tip #2: Put things in perspective. What you're doing with apartment building investing is hard. It's definitely worthwhile, but it's really hard. It's not like you can get the results you want (replacing your income) in thirty days or less. No, you have to stick with it—every week for three to five years until you can quit your job and do what you really want.

While this is a *really* long time, look at it from this perspective: your retirement plan is only three to five years. Most people have a forty-plus year retirement plan, but yours is only three to five years. Isn't that much better? So if you're considering giving up after three months of doing this apartment building investing thing, think about the time line you're on. You know that you're on a three-to-five-year

---

4   "Tony Robbins Quotes," BrainyQuote, accessed January 24, 2018, https://www.brainyquote.com/quotes/tony_robbins_147787.

retirement plan, so clearly three months isn't going to cut it. But you also know that your retirement time line is infinitely *better* and *faster* than 99% of other people out there, so it's definitely worth it.

Okay, enough complaining. Get back to working the plan!

Tip #3: Recognize and celebrate your (small) successes. I find in working with students that they often don't see the progress they're making. They're so focused on doing their first deal (as they should be!) that when it doesn't happen in the first few months, they become discouraged. In reality, they've made tremendous progress, and it's important to recognize this by celebrating the small successes.

Here are some examples of small successes you should celebrate (and why they're important):

- **You analyzed ten deals:** This is huge because it demonstrates that you stuck with it. Anyone can analyze a few deals, but ten shows persistence. Good for you! Another reason this milestone is important is because after analyzing about ten deals, your confidence level increases substantially, which makes this a meaningful milestone.

- **You submitted your first Letter of Intent:** If you've read this far, then you know by now that whenever you analyze a deal, you're also making a 10-Minute Offer, which is an informal offer. If you get a reaction from the seller, such as a counter-offer, or you're asked to put your offer in writing, you then submit a Letter of Intent. Being asked to submit an LOI assumes that you probably made a dozen or even several dozen 10-Minute Offers—that's a huge accomplishment in itself. Then you convinced a broker that he should take you seriously, which means you probably have a compelling team and a higher level of confidence. In other words, being asked to submit an LOI is a huge milestone, and you should celebrate it lavishly!

- **You've had your first investor meeting:** If you've convinced someone to meet you for an hour to discuss investing with you, that means you must have reached out to at least a dozen or so people in your network and had conversations with many of them about your apartment building investing ambitions. A *lot* of preparation and activity went into that first investor meeting—ring the bell!

- **Your team is in place:** Have you interviewed and identified your favorite property manager and commercial mortgage broker? If so, then this is a huge milestone. These two team members are going to be key as you analyze deals and make offers. Without them, you are literally flying blind. Recognize and celebrate this accomplishment!

- **You got your first investor commitment:** Your brother-in-law said he was in for $50K? Don't gloss over this—this is huge! Not only did a lot of activity precede this milestone, but you made someone else comfortable with investing with you. They're taking you seriously. Nice job! And this first commitment really boosts your confidence as you approach your other investors. It's now much easier to find that second and third investor than the first. You're now well on your way to raising ALL the money you need for your first deal. Keep it up!

- **You have your first deal under contract:** Just because you got an LOI signed doesn't mean you'll get it under contract. An LOI is not a legally binding document, and many brokers and sellers treat it that way while they're negotiating with their *real* buyer. Many times, the devil is in the details, and you and the seller might not agree on the terms of the deal as they're spelled out in the contract. Getting a deal under contract also means that you made the seller comfortable with you, your team, and your ability to close. This milestone is huge. Take the family out for dinner!

Stick with It!

The key to surviving the "graveyard of apartment building investing" is, first and foremost, awareness. Anticipate the feelings of doubt and discouragement as you experience setbacks, challenges, and delays. This is where an accountability partner or mentor is key, because they will guide you through these days of doubt and discouragement. They will put these feelings into perspective, remind you of your goals, highlight the progress you've already made, and encourage you to keep going.

The good news is that if you can get over this three-month hump, you're good to go. Just be aware of it, surround yourself with good support, and keep on moving forward.

CHAPTER 12

Step #6: Milestones to Closing Your First Deal

If you continue to consistently analyze deals, meet with investors, and build your team, you *will* develop a pipeline of deals and get commitments from investors. And once you have a pipeline of deals and investors, it's only a matter of time until you do your first deal.

In this chapter, I want to outline the process of closing your first deal. I'm saying "outline" because I could write another 200 pages on this topic, but it would be a major distraction to the main point of this book, which is how to become financially free with real estate.

I don't want to overwhelm you with details about the closing process. There is a *lot* to learn about getting a property under contract, doing due diligence, raising money, hiring and managing your property manager, and so forth. But instead of going into gruesome detail about the closing process, I will hit the high points of each milestone and then point you to additional resources in the free Companion Course, so that you have more information if you're interested.

There are eight major milestones to closing your first deal:

1. Negotiate and Ratify the Contract
2. Perform Due Diligence

3. Hire Your Property Manager

4. Secure Financing

5. Initiate the Closing Process

6. Prepare Your Investors for Closing

7. Close and Cash Your Acquisition Fee Check

8. Manage the Property for Maximum Profits

Okay, let's jump right into the first milestone, which is to negotiate and ratify the purchase contract.

CHAPTER 13

Milestone #1: Negotiate and Ratify the Contract

Once you have the Letter of Intent signed by both parties, it's time to draft the Purchase and Sales Agreement (PSA). Typically, the seller's attorney will provide you with the first draft, but if you can negotiate it so that your attorney provides it, that's even better!

Regardless of which attorney provides the PSA, make sure these major terms are addressed in the contract.

3 Priceless Contract Negotiation Tips to Keep You in Control of the Deal

Tip #1: Use days, not dates. Most contracts use dates to define important milestones, such as the day due diligence expires or when the closing is scheduled. But what if something happens that causes you or the other party to miss a particular date? It should push all dates following that date back, right? But if your contract is written with hard dates, that won't happen.

Let's say you negotiated that the seller is to deliver a certified survey to you within the next four weeks (which also corresponds to the expiration of the due diligence period) and that the closing date will be May 1 (seventy-five days after ratifying the contract). But what if the seller doesn't deliver the survey to you? Would this automatically push back the closing date?

No, it wouldn't, which would mean that you would still need to close May 1, even if the delays were caused by the seller. Since you couldn't close May 1, you would be in default of the contract, and that might mean that you would lose your deposit.

Not good.

The solution to this problem is to use the number of days *after* an event occurs instead of absolute dates on the calendar. So, instead of saying you will close May 1, you would say that you would close sixty days after the expiration of the due diligence period, which is either four weeks from contract ratification or the date you receive the survey, whichever comes later. Now the seller could drag their feet as long as they wanted to, you would continue to control the property, and closing would be sixty days after the seller delivers the survey.

So, make sure you don't use absolute dates in your contract!

Tip #2: Properly define the length of your due diligence period. This is similar to Tip #1 in that it relates to the use of absolute time frames. When buying a property, many investors make the mistake of defining their due diligence period in terms of just the number of days from the signing of the contract.

Let's say the contract gives you thirty days for due diligence. But what if it takes the seller fourteen days to deliver all of the due diligence documents? Then you would only have two weeks to research the property! Can you complete your due diligence in the next fourteen days? Probably not. And you shouldn't have to.

Instead of defining due diligence as "thirty days after contract ratification," define it as thirty days after receipt of all documentation. Then, if the seller takes two weeks to deliver everything, you still have the full thirty days after that to complete due diligence.

Tip #3: Include at least one contract extension. Remember that you want to stay in control of the transaction even if things happen that are out of your control.

Let's say you agreed to closing sixty days after the expiration of the due diligence period, but your bank needs more time to complete the underwriting process. Now, two things can happen:

1. You need the seller to give you an extension (which they may or may not grant you), or

2. You're in default of the contract, and you lose your deposit.

Either option is undesirable.

Instead, build in a thirty-day contract extension option that you can exercise at your discretion by paying an additional 0.25% or 0.5% of the purchase price deposit into escrow. Most sellers won't mind if this is in your contract, and it can save you big time later on. If your lender needs an extra fourteen days to approve the financing, you can exercise this option and stay under contract and in control.

Interestingly, one of the major fears from newbie apartment entrepreneurs is that their offer gets accepted—especially if the entrepreneur hasn't raised all of the money yet. This fear stops these investors from making offers.

Before moving on to the next milestone (performing due diligence), let me show you that you don't need to be afraid of getting your offers accepted.

Don't Be Afraid of Success

Susan was an enthusiastic student. She did what she was told and consistently analyzed deals and talked to potential investors. Yet for some reason, she wasn't making any offers, even though her analysis was sound. After a couple of coaching sessions, I asked her about this, and she said she wasn't making offers because she didn't have all of the money raised. She didn't want to make any offers because if it was accepted, she wouldn't be able to close the deal.

I've found that she wasn't the only one who felt this way, so I want to address this fear first. If you can't overcome this fear early on, you won't make any offers and of course, if you don't make any offers, it's tough to close your first deal, right?

This "fear of success" keeps many newbie multifamily investors on the sidelines. They've been looking for deals while trying to raise money from private individuals. They come across a good deal but don't have all of the funds committed yet.

And they STOP pursuing the deal.

Because they're afraid.

This is a mistake for at least TWO reasons:

- **They underestimate the value of a good underwritten and pre-negotiated deal.** Especially these days, finding good multifamily deals is tough. So when you have a deal that you have at least verbal agreement from the seller on a number that makes sense after rigorous and conservative underwriting, you have something of value.

Even if you DON'T end up closing on the deal, there will be a LONG line of people who would die to get their hands on a deal like that.

- **You should always walk through open doors until they close.** In my eleven years of being a full-time entrepreneur, I have learned that the universe gives you opportunities all the time. Many times, we don't see them or, more frequently, we fail to take advantage of them because we're afraid.

I have found that when we walk through the open door presented to us, magical things happen, things we never thought possible. Therefore, I'd like to share this rule with you: if a door opens that is aligned with your purpose and goals, you should keep walking through that door until it's permanently closed. Don't give up until then.

The "Worst Case Scenario" Exercise

Sometimes we fail to do something because we're afraid of what COULD happen.

Even if the likelihood of that happening is remote.

One exercise I like to do when I'm afraid is to write down all of the "bad" things that could happen if that fear were realized. I find that once I see the potential outcomes on paper, they don't seem that bad, and my fear becomes manageable to the point where I can continue to take action.

Let's do that exercise for the following situation:

Let's assume you found a 15-unit apartment building, analyzed it, and made an offer. The seller countered, so you sharpened your pencil and continued to negotiate a price that works.

It's actually a smokin' hot deal.

But you need about $250,000 in cash to close on this deal; you've only raised $50,000 of it from friends and family.

Let's further assume that you choose to continue walking through the open door. You decide to submit a Letter of Intent.

In the time it takes to negotiate and sign the Letter of Intent, you have three to five extra days to call potential investors.

You also decide to work on Plan B, which is to call other potential investors who might be interested in buying this deal from you. You could partner with them, refer the deal to them, or wholesale the deal to them.

You call brokers, property managers, and other professionals who might be able to put you in touch with owners of similar buildings. You network at your local REIA or on sites like Bigger Pockets to look for people who already own multifamily buildings like this.

You get the Letter of Intent signed. You now have seven business days to submit a purchase contract. Getting the contract ratified takes another five days. You now have an extra two weeks to raise money or find another buyer or partner.

Now you have twenty-one days to complete due diligence. This gives you at least an extra two weeks to raise the money or find another buyer.

Since submitting the LOI, you've had almost an entire month to raise the extra money or to find someone else who would assume the contract. This is probably more time than you realized!

You have a good deal, and plenty of people are either looking for somewhere to put their cash or to buy a multifamily building that has been hard to find.

Worst case, if despite all of these efforts you FAIL to raise the money or find a single person who wants the deal you've delivered to them on a silver platter, you can always exercise the due diligence termination clause in your contract.

If you construct your contract correctly, you can terminate the contract for ANY reason before the due diligence period expires.

(While you can exercise this clause for ANY reason whatsoever, I would caution you to either have a GOOD reason or at least try to preserve the respect of the broker. Otherwise, you will quickly develop the reputation for "not closing" and wasting everyone's time).

What's the Lesson?

Once you complete this "worst case" exercise, you can see that your "worst" case isn't really that bad after all. That's Lesson #1.

And Lesson #2 is to keep moving forward through open doors until they're permanently closed. I have found time and again that magical things happen when you do.

Okay, now that we have that out of the way, I hope you're making offers! And when you do, eventually one of them will get accepted.

Additional Resources

Please access the Companion Course for these additional resources related to the contract negotiation process:

- *How to Know It's Time to Walk Away from an Apartment Building Deal:* You've looked at many different apartment building deals, and you finally have one under contract. Congratulations! Now the real work begins: due diligence. If you don't uncover anything new that materially changes the deal, you're well on your way to closing. However, many times you DO uncover things during due diligence that you weren't told about up-front or that you just didn't know. This resource includes four tips to help you decide when it's time to walk away.

- *Negotiating 101: The Importance of Agreeing on Methodology BEFORE Making an Offer:* This article covers the first tip needed for successful real estate negotiation. You really don't want to miss this!

- *The Power of Using Video for Negotiating Apartment Deals:* Get more of your apartment deals accepted through the power of using video!

- *The Step-by-Step Guide to Making Offers on Apartment Buildings:* How do you define "making an offer" on commercial real estate, and what's the process? I've put together a detailed step-by-step guide!

To access these resources, go to FinancialFreedomTheBook.com/course > Chapter 13: Negotiate and Ratify the Contract.

Once both parties have executed the Purchase and Sales Agreement, you're officially under contract. Now the real fun begins!

CHAPTER 14

Milestone #2: Perform Due Diligence

You have an apartment building under contract, which is awesome. Performing due diligence is an exciting part of the buying process. It means you successfully negotiated the deal (which is not easy to do!) and you're ready to start due diligence to determine if it's a deal you want to close.

Many investors are so eager that they begin spending money during the diligence process before they should, and they unnecessarily put cash at risk that they'll never get back if they decide not to close.

Don't make that mistake.

Delay spending money as long as possible.

For example, don't hire a property inspector to inspect the property (which costs money) *before* reviewing the financials (which is free). Review the due diligence documents *first* before spending any money.

The Checklist That Can Help You Save Big During Due Diligence

Here is my due diligence checklist in the right order to make sure you're not spending money until you are 99% sure you're going to close on this building. The following checklist assumes you have a

21-day due diligence period—adjust accordingly if your inspection period is different.

Week One

- Send a letter to the seller requesting financial and other due diligence documents.

- Informally tour the property and inspect some of the units with your property manager or contractor.

- Perform a rent survey.

- If you have investors, create the deal package for them.

- Request term sheets from your lenders.

- Request insurance quotes.

Notice that *no money has been spent yet.*

Week Two

- Review the documents you received from the seller and reevaluate the deal.

- Update your deal analyzer with the financials you received from the seller. Incorporate the repair estimates from your initial property visit. Does the deal still make sense?

- If so, complete the deal package and send it to your investors. You'd like verbal commitments from them next week.

Week Three

- Order the initial title report to see if there are any title issues.

- Decide which property manager you're going to hire.

- Get verbal commitments from your investors.

If you still like the deal, it's time to consider a formal property inspection (which may be the first money you spend). Sometimes your property management company will do this for you for free or for a fee, or you may choose to hire a professional inspection company. Whatever your choice, you want them to inspect every unit and all of the major systems, and then create a detailed report that you can give to your contractor for a cost estimate.

If you're in an area where lead paint laws are an important consideration, then you should also order a lead paint inspection.

The main point is this: delay spending money as long as possible.

Even though you may have had to spend some money on a property inspection, you did so only *after* reviewing the financials and only *after* touring the property yourself.

If the inspection uncovered significant issues, then it was money well spent. If not, you can feel confident about going to closing. If you still feel good about moving forward, there is more money that needs to be spent before you close: for example, you will need to pay a deposit to the lender or bank to order the appraisal. You may also need to pay your attorney to draft the Operating Agreement or a Private Placement Memorandum.

Before spending this kind of money, you want to have a high degree of confidence that you want to move forward with the deal.

Follow this guideline, and you will minimize the money you risk during the due diligence process.

The Biggest Mistake I Almost Made Buying an Apartment Building (And What You Can Learn from It)

I want to share with you the biggest mistake I almost made when buying an apartment building. Had I made this mistake, I most surely would have lost the building in foreclosure within several months. And despite all of my education, training, and reading, this is something none of the experts warned me about.

Once I got this building under contract and it was time for due diligence, I requested the following documentation from the seller: utility bills, invoices, service contracts, leases, rent roll, tax returns, etc. Her documentation was woefully incomplete, but I did have the rent roll and a copy of the leases. The building currently had a 15% vacancy, but I was told that this was a temporary condition and that it's normally full. Okay, whatever ... I had still underwritten the deal with 15% vacancy.

It then occurred to me that I should try to verify the rents she was collecting. What could be worse than a bunch of tenants not paying their rent, right? I asked for a copy of her tax return for the building that shows actual income. She didn't have it or didn't want to give it to me.

I then asked for bank statements that show the rental deposits. After about a week, the broker faxed over bank statements, but they looked like personal bank statements. I had no clue what deposits were from rents, so I asked her to highlight the relevant ones.

This, of course, took another week. When I got the highlights back and added up the deposits for the last six months, it looked like she was really only collecting 50% of the rent.

What? HALF the tenants aren't paying their rent? Are you kidding?

So let me get this straight: after I close, not only will I collect only half the rent but I'll then need to spend thousands of dollars in legal fees to evict these tenants, then spend another several thousand dollars to turn the units over. I asked the seller about this, and she said that these were tough times for the tenants, but they were good tenants and they would pay, they'd just fallen behind the last few months.

For me, the building was now only worth HALF of what I had it under contract for. I proposed three options to the seller:

1. Drop the contract price by half (which wasn't likely to happen);

2. Add a contingency to give her time to collect at least 90% of the rent for a period of three months in a row and I had the right to review any new tenants she brings in; or

3. She guarantees me a year's worth of rents from any of her tenants who didn't pay.

None of these options worked for her (as expected), and so we terminated the contract. Three weeks later, the broker contacted me and said that she wanted to pursue the third option.

She paid a large amount of money into an escrow account that was administered by an escrow agent, and every time one of her tenants didn't pay rent, I would get the difference from this escrow account. This allowed me to stabilize the property over the next twelve months.

Lessons Learned

One lesson, of course, is to be creative in coming up with solutions that work for both you and the seller. Ask for the delinquency number up front and make sure you add some amount of bad debt to your underwriting; and then, most importantly, **verify the actual rental deposits during due diligence**.

I find it so interesting that as I review new deals, the delinquency factor is rarely listed on a broker's marketing package. They'll have vacancies, of course, and maybe concessions and loss to lease, but very rarely do I see the line item called "bad debt." That's a fancy phrase for "uncollected rent." Very often, this number can be significant.

Follow the due diligence checklist to the letter, don't cut corners, and verify the income. Otherwise, you might get a very unpleasant surprise once you own the building.

Speaking of mistakes, I interviewed Brian Hennessey about the subject of due diligence mistakes on Podcast #29. Brian has been in commercial real estate for thirty-one years and is the author of the book *The Due Diligence Handbook for Commercial Real Estate*. He's done over 9 million square feet of sale transactions, and in the process, he's learned some valuable lessons. In other words, he knows a little something about due diligence.

Here is his summary of the top ten most common mistakes to avoid when purchasing an investment property opportunity:

Mistake #1: Not valuing the property correctly. Make sure you're conservative in your underwriting of a deal. Do your homework! That means checking for sales comps and other available properties on the market. Contact the more active commercial brokers in the area and inquire about local property values and sale comparables. Then continue to adjust your valuation during the due diligence based on what you find.

Mistake #2: Not understanding your lender's underwriting requirements. Before you spend a lot of time, money, and energy conducting your due diligence, make sure you've had a preliminary discussion with some lenders about the amount of the loan they would consider putting on the property. Today's lenders are very conservative and look at many aspects of the property such as: physical condition, sale and lease comparables, leases in place, intended use, environmental issues, credit worthiness of purchaser, etc. Check with them before you get too far down the road with your due diligence to avoid surprises later.

Mistake #3: Not checking if the property complies with all current municipal building codes. It's a fairly common occurrence that a buyer finds out after purchasing a property that it doesn't meet the compliance of building and/or ADA codes. This comes up when the contractor goes to pull a permit from the city for intended improvements or when the city inspector comes out to check out the contractor's work, discovering the infractions. Be sure to keep an eye out for tenants whose space has been built-out without a permit. It's a good idea to have a contractor, architect, or space planner inspect the property to discuss any improvements and compliance during your due diligence period. You don't want any costly surprises after the closing.

Mistake #4: Assuming there are no issues within existing tenant leases. The leases can have many "trip wires" such as cancellation provisions, contraction provisions, caps on pass-through expenses, fixed option rents—just to name a few. You want to be aware of these provisions because if the tenant exercises them, it could put you in a bind and devalue the property. It's important to have a competent real estate attorney read the leases if you are not familiar with commercial real estate leasing.

Mistake #5: Assuming lenders will accept all third-party reports. Before hiring any third-party vendors to conduct an inspection and prepare a report, make sure that your lender approves them. This goes for the Property Condition Assessment, Environmental Reports, or any specialized reports—such as seismic or geological studies. Mistakenly having to pay two different vendors for the same report costs much more than time; it is very expensive.

Mistake #6: Trusting that the seller and their representative have disclosed all issues. You have to be a detective when performing your investigation/due diligence on a property you're looking to purchase. Not all sellers are going to be forthcoming with disclosing the problems of their property. Remember the Latin saying, *caveat emptor*: let the buyer beware. Ask the hard questions and make sure you do that in writing (i.e., email them so you can keep track and record all correspondence in case you need to bring it to court one day). Always ask for backup receipts, lien releases, copies of paid invoices, etc. Remember, ASSUME NOTHING.

Mistake #7: Expecting the closing statement to be without issues. Before you sign the final approval of the closing statement sent by the escrow officer, be sure you have scrutinized all the items listed, as well as those omitted. Many times, a seller will load up items to be credited to themselves and "forget" items that should be credited to the buyer.

Some commonly overlooked items are: letters of credit or Certificates of Deposit used as security from tenants that the landlord needs to assign to the new buyer, leasing commissions owed to brokers on leases that have recently been signed, tenant improvement allowances owed to tenants, vendor billings that need to be prorated or paid in full prior to new ownership taking over.

Mistake #8: Not checking out the competition. You need to keep an eye on your competition, especially if you're not familiar with the area. If you see rent specials or other concessions, you need to know they exist and why, because they might affect your underwriting and valuation of the deal.

Mistake #9: Not spending time at the property. Go there at different times of the day. You're going to get a much better idea of what goes on there. That parking lot might be a hangout for kids to party on the weekends. You get a chance to speak with the tenants. Seeing the place in a different light might even change your mind about the property.

Mistake #10: Not walking each and every unit. Even if the seller doesn't want to disrupt the tenants, this is essential. You want to see every unit in person. You don't know what they're going to be hiding. Maybe one of the units has mold or fire issues—you can't know unless you inspect it yourself. Insist on it.

Conclusion

Many new commercial real estate investors don't know what they don't know, and hopefully this list will help with that. Also make sure you follow your due diligence checklist, and don't cut corners.

In summary, don't underestimate the importance of due diligence. A deal you passed on is much better than a deal you made, only to find out later it was a mistake.

Additional Resources

Please access the Companion Course for these additional resources related to the due diligence process:

- *Estimating Acquisition and Closing Costs for Apartment Building Deals:* In this article I review some rules of thumb for estimating your acquisition and closing costs, which many investors underestimate.

- *4 Steps to Perform a Rent Survey for Your Investment Property:* Are you missing out on rent money or pricing your units too high to fill? Find out critical information for your business plan by taking these steps.

To access these resources, go to FinancialFreedomTheBook.com/course > Chapter 14: Perform Due Diligence.

Now that you know you're going to move forward with the deal, it's time to hire your property manager.

CHAPTER 15

Milestone #3: Hire Your Property Manager

Hiring a property manager is probably the most important decision you will make (aside from actually buying the building). The success of the project depends on the quality of your property manager. A good manager will make your life easy; a bad one ... well, not so much.

Not only will they manage the property for you, but they also play a key role during due diligence, because a good property manager will help you assess your business plan for the property.

The best way to find property managers is to ask for referrals, primarily from your real estate brokers, who should know at least a handful of good property managers.

But how do you recognize the good ones? Here are three steps for selecting the best property management company for your property:

Step #1: How to Interview the Property Manager (and What to Look for)

Here are ten questions to ask your potential property manager and what to look for:

1. **How long have you been in business?** I'm always in favor of giving the upstart a chance; so you might want to consider someone you like with only a year of experience in the business. But in general, the longer they've been around, the better.

2. **What size properties do you manage the most?** If you're looking to purchase a 4-plex building, don't interview a company that specializes in 100-unit buildings. Processes and procedures are totally different for these types of buildings.

3. **What are your management fees for my size building?** What is your leasing fee? How else are you compensated? Management fees generally range from 5% for larger properties to 10% for smaller properties. Leasing fees range from a half month to a full month rent. The only other type of compensation is a mark-up for repairs (typically, 10%).

4. **What is your process for handling repair requests?** How do tenants make requests? How quickly do you typically respond? Who does the work? What do you charge for the work? You're looking for a well-defined process. Preferably, tenants can log in online to make the request. This gives you transparency into the process regarding response times and any communication between the tenant and property manager. The property manager should have a network of contractors to handle any repairs at the property. They typically charge 10% over and above what the contractor charges for the repair. How are emergency and non-business hour calls handled? How do they ensure that their prices continue to be competitive over time?

5. **How do you collect rents? Who keeps the late fees?** Offering automatic debit, for example, shows a higher level of

sophistication than someone who collects the rents in person. The late fees go to the managers, they're split, or they all go to you—this is negotiable, just know this upfront.

6. **What are your management policies (e.g., when and how do you handle lease violations and evictions)?** You're looking for a fair and consistent process. For example, the manager might say, "The rent is considered late on the fifth day of the month, at which point I will send out a late rent letter warning them they have until the twenty-first day of the month to pay, or we will start the eviction process. I then file the eviction on the twenty-second day if no payment is made. I will continue to communicate with the tenant through the entire process." That is a sign of fair and consistent management policy.

7. **How many evictions have you handled, and what is the cost of a typical eviction?** The more evictions, the more experience. The cost varies widely by region, so make sure you ask. Update your financial analysis accordingly.

8. What is the expected vacancy and delinquency rate for this area? Update your financial analysis accordingly.

9. **What reports do you provide?** At a minimum, you should expect an income and expense statement and a rent roll each month—both are typical. You also want to see any delinquencies. For extra credit, you could ask for a repair and maintenance report that documents the description, cost, and turnaround time for every repair made.

10. **How do you handle the funds?** Will you get a separate bank account? This is preferable, but many property managers don't do this for properties under twenty-five units. The advantage of

a separate account is that you can get a monthly bank statement in addition to the income/expense statement, which gives additional visibility into how your money is being handled. What reserve does he or she require? Typically, the manager will require a certain minimum in the bank account and will forward any excess to you.

Be sure to interview at least three property management companies. That will give you more of a feel of what to look for and help you decide which company you like best.

Step #2: Review the Manager's Documents

At the end of your meeting, ask the manager to send you a sample of his or her contracts (leases, late letters, etc.) and accounting reports. Also request a list of references.

Step #3: Check References

If you like what you've heard so far, call the references. Ask the following questions:

1. How pleased are you with the manager?
2. What is he or she doing particularly well?
3. What is one thing he or she could improve?
4. Why would you recommend your manager?

Step #4: Review the Property Management Agreement

Read the management agreement carefully, as sometimes there are clauses to be cautious about. For example, in one of my contracts it states that the property manager has thirty days to exercise a first right of refusal to purchase the property; but I don't want the manager to delay a contract for that period of time. This is just an example—the point is, read the management contract in detail, as you should any contract.

Next Steps

Now that you have all the information about this property manager, it's time for a gut check. Sometimes a person looks good on paper, but your instinct is telling you otherwise. Look at all the pros and cons, but at the end of day, go with your gut. Make a decision and adjust later if necessary.

Once you give the keys to the manager after closing, the company should communicate to the tenants that there is a new manager in charge. They will likely communicate a new mailing address for the checks, and they may include a new rules and regulations booklet.

Be aware that bringing on a new manager may cause several tenants to stop paying their rent. My theory is that these tenants are testing the new manager to see what they can get away with. How the manager responds (quickly, consistently, and fairly) will determine the level of respect they will get from the tenants.

Additional Property Management Resources

Please access the Companion Course for these additional resources related to hiring the property management company:

- *Before You Attempt to Manage Your Own Property, Answer These 5 Questions:* Thinking about self-managing your investment properties? Read this first ... you may change your mind!

- *MB 015: How to Find the Best Property Manager with Jake Durtschi:* In this episode I ask Jake Durtschi with Jacob Grant Property Management 101 interview questions to help you select the best property manager.

To access these resources, go to FinancialFreedomTheBook.com/course > Chapter 15: Hire Your Property Manager.

Now that you've hired your property management company, let's move on to our next milestone: securing financing.

CHAPTER 16

Milestone #4: Secure Financing

Before you put an apartment building deal under contract, you should clearly understand your potential lenders' loan terms and underwriting criteria. Otherwise, you might put a deal under contract and assume a down payment of 20%, only to find out later that you'll need to put 30% down, or that you don't personally qualify for the loan and need to find a co-sponsor, or that the lender requires a six-month reserve that you didn't count on.

While ignorance is sometimes bliss, in this case, these kinds of surprises could cost you a deal. And when you're doing a deal, you don't want surprises like these. The lesson learned is this: clearly understand the terms of the potential loan and how the lender will underwrite the deal. Remember, *underwrite* is a fancy term that refers to how the lender assesses the risk of a project, what they require of you as the sponsor to mitigate those risks, how it satisfies their lending guidelines, and the ultimate terms of the loan.

To understand your lender's underwriting criteria, make sure you network with potential mortgage brokers or lenders long *before* you start making offers on deals.

But what do lenders look for? And what questions should you ask?

In this section, I will share the most common underwriting

requirements and terms you can expect from a commercial lender, and also how you can satisfy their lending requirements, even if you don't qualify yourself.

What Lenders Look for in a Borrower

As you meet with loan brokers or lenders, give them multiple scenarios and ask what they are likely to require to approve the loan and what the terms would be. What would the terms look like for a stabilized asset? What about one that is a distressed value-add deal? What would a bridge loan look like?

Here are some of the key loan terms and underwriting requirements and what to look for:

Debt Coverage Ratio

This is the ratio of your debt service payment to the net operating income. For a stable asset, the lender will look for a ratio of 1.25 or higher. If it's a value-add deal with little cash flow in the first year, for example, they may relax this requirement in return for an interest reserve at closing.

Loan to Value

This is the ratio of the loan balance to the value of the asset. For a stabilized asset in good areas, banks will lend up to 80% of the value. I use 75% in my projections and even lower if the property is not stabilized.

Net Worth

Lenders are looking for a net worth of the sponsors that are equal to or greater than the loan amount. If your personal net worth does not meet these requirements, partner with someone who's willing to sign the note with you. Offer that partner some additional equity in the deal, or pay him or her a fee at closing.

Liquidity

Lenders like to see liquidity among the sponsors of 10% of the loan balance. Typically, they don't require you to keep this in a separate account—they just want to see that level of liquidity in the sponsors' personal financial statement. If you have a partner signing the note with you, then the bank will also consider that person's liquidity.

Personal Guarantees

Banks like personal guarantees. Loans that need to be personally guaranteed are also called "recourse." This means that if you were to default, the bank could go after your personal assets.

You want to avoid personal guarantees in general, not only for yourself, but also for any investors you have involved in the deal. Your investors are typically "limited partners" with limited decision-making authority, and they're not investing with you to take on any more liability than potentially losing their principal.

For loan amounts under $1M, the banks generally want a personal guarantee. Interestingly, the higher the loan amount, the more likely you will get a nonrecourse loan—another reason to try to go BIG as soon as possible!

You can negotiate personal guarantees (and other terms of the note). For example, you might be able to "bleed off" the guarantee, which means that the amount of the guarantee decreases over the years.

Bridge loans normally require a personal guarantee but then can go away once the asset has been stabilized.

As a syndicator, I am mostly concerned about the recourse, net worth, and liquidity requirements, because my personal financial statement may not support the kind of asset that I'm looking for now. This means I, too, will have to partner with someone to make up for this "shortcoming."

Keep these key points in mind:

- **Partner!** You don't need to limit yourself to your own personal financial statement. If you're "weak" there, partner up! Find one of your investors who complements your net worth and liquidity requirements.

- **Go big as quickly as possible** You don't want to have to personally guarantee a bunch of buildings, do you? Limit your personal liability as much as possible, negotiate the loan documents. Also shoot for bigger assets so that you get non-recourse loans.

- **Talk to your lenders EARLY.** Be in touch with lenders long before you have your deal under contract so that you better understand their underwriting requirements. This allows you to get your ducks in a row ahead of time so that you can close on your deals.

As with most things in business, it's all about relationships. Build a relationship with your lenders *now* so that when you really need them, they'll come through for you.

The Top 10 Questions You Need to Ask Your Commercial Mortgage Broker

In your interview with your commercial mortgage broker, ask them these ten questions:

1. What are the basic terms I can expect for a typical loan? Specifically, what loan-to-value (LTV), interest rate, term, and amortization can I expect?

2. Is the loan nonrecourse, or does it have to be personally guaranteed?

3. What are the costs of the loan? Specifically, what are the origination fees (typically, 1% of the loan), and what is the cost of third-party reports, such as the appraisal, structural and environmental reports, and legal fees?

4. What size loans do you typically do, and in what areas?

5. What are the prepayment penalties if you decide to refinance or sell before the term of the loan?

6. What are your liquidity and net worth requirements? Typically, the lender will require the sponsor(s) to show liquidity of 10% of the loan and a net worth equal to the loan balance.

7. Do you require any reserves or minimum account balances? Some lenders want you to deposit six to nine months of interest payments into an escrow account and/or keep a minimum balance in the bank account. Some also want you to bank with them as a condition of the loan.

8. What is the typical time to close from the time I order the appraisal? Normally, loans take forty-five to sixty days from the time the appraisal is ordered to close. Make sure you know the time frame for this lender.

9. How do you define a "stable" asset? Typically, assets that are at least 80% occupied are considered "stable" and anything less occupied is considered "distressed." If you're talking to this lender about a conventional loan for a "stable" asset, make sure you know what they consider "stable."

10. What kind of loan products do you provide? Lenders could provide one or more of these loans: conventional, Fannie Mae/Freddie Mac, FHA/HUD, bridge, and/or construction loans. The more products a broker can provide, the better.

Keep copious notes, and then add the answers to a spreadsheet where you track the nuances and terms for each lender. Do this for three to five lenders and you'll get a good idea of what's "normal" and what might be a bit unusual.

Now that you have the answers to all of these questions, you will better understand your lender's requirements to ensure you qualify for the loan, and you know the actual terms. Therefore, once you have a deal under contract and time is of the essence, you already have a relationship with the broker, know what terms to expect, and are confident that you have a very good chance of being approved. Following these steps will dramatically increase your chances of closing the deal.

Now that we understand our lenders' requirements, let's review the loan process and timing.

The Loan Process and Timing

The first step in the loan process is to complete a loan application and provide preliminary information about yourself and the deal.

Once you have a deal under contract, you want a term sheet from your loan officer as quickly as possible. A *term sheet* is a short one- or two-page letter that outlines the main terms of the loan, pending final underwriting. You can use the term sheet to compare different lenders with each other and select the best terms for you. I've found that the lenders take one to two weeks to produce a term sheet from the time they get the Deal Package from you.

After you receive the term sheet, the ball is in your court. The next step is for you to select your lender, which involves you ordering and paying for an appraisal. Normally, the bank will require you to pay a non-refundable deposit that will cover the cost of the appraisal, and maybe a few other things. The amount of this deposit is negotiable to some extent, but banks tend to be set in their fee structures.

The appraisal typically takes twenty-one to thirty days (I still don't understand why it takes this long). Once it's completed, your loan will enter final underwriting, which takes another one to two weeks. The outcome of this process is a commitment letter that is a definite "yes" to the loan and its terms. Normally the terms are substantially the same as the term sheet, unless the underwriter discovers things about the deal he or she doesn't like and adjusts the terms accordingly.

Once you receive the commitment letter from the underwriter, it takes another fourteen to twenty-one days to close.

While there are always exceptions, plan for the bank to take at least forty-five days to close once you order the appraisal (and most lenders would prefer sixty days).

Additional Resources

Please access the Companion Course for these additional resources related to securing financing:

- *How to Use a Master Lease to Acquire Commercial Real Estate with No Money Down:* We covered conventional financing in this chapter, but what about more creative financing? Using a master lease can be a GREAT way to acquire commercial real estate with no money down. Learn the ins and outs here!

To access this resource, go to FinancialFreedomTheBook.com/course > Chapter 16: Secure Financing.

Now that you've picked your favorite lender and understand their requirements and the loan process, it's time to kick off the closing process.

CHAPTER 17

Milestone #5: Initiate the Closing Process

If you made it this far, there's a good chance you're happy with the deal and want to (gulp) move forward. You've completed your due diligence, and the only thing that would stand between you and closing on the deal is financing and shepherding your investors to wire the funds into escrow.

So far, we've deferred spending a lot of money (except perhaps traveling to the property and the formal inspection), but now it's time to spend some real money. And if you don't close, you want to recover the money you're about to spend. However, if you've followed the process up to this point, you should feel confident that you'll be able to close and get reimbursed for these due diligence expenses.

Now that the due diligence period has expired, you will instruct the closing attorney to start title work, order the appraisal with your lender, and pay a retainer for your attorney to draft various legal documents.

Follow these steps to initiate the closing process:

Step #1: Instruct the Closing Attorney to Order the Title Report

Contact the closing attorney and instruct her or him to begin title work and initiate the closing process. You should not incur any fees from this activity until closing. Some closing attorneys advise that the title work be ordered earlier in the due diligence process because it could take longer in some jurisdictions. Listen to your team of advisors!

Step #2: Choose Your Lender and Order the Appraisal

In the previous milestone we talked about understanding the underwriting requirements of multiple lenders. During due diligence, you will have requested and received term sheets from at least three lenders and selected your favorite. Now it's time to reach out to that lender and give them the green light to proceed. Typically, that lender will require you to make a deposit to pay for the appraisal. Go ahead and send in that check to get the ball rolling.

Step #3: Instruct the Attorney to Create the Entity and Draft Legal Documents

Now that you know you're proceeding with the closing, it's time to create the LLC (or other entity) that will take title of the property.

You'll likely need to pay your attorney a retainer to begin drafting your LLC Operating Agreement and Private Placement Memorandum (if you have investors). Let the attorney know when your closing date is to make sure he can get the documents done in time. Typically, at this point of the process, you have about forty-five to sixty days to close (the amount of time the bank normally requires from the time you order the appraisal).

Because the Operating Agreement and Private Placement Memorandum are such hefty documents, you'll spend quite a bit of time reviewing and revising them for the attorney.

Once you've kicked off the loan process and instructed the attorneys to begin closing, you can focus on the next step, which is to prepare the investors for closing.

CHAPTER 18

Milestone #6: Prepare Your Investors for Closing

Once you've ordered the appraisal and instructed the attorney to draft the legal documents, your main activity until closing is to provide the lender with documents they request and to prepare the investors for closing. Before we get into the closing logistics, let's review the entity and SEC-compliance documentation that your SEC attorney will create for you during this step.

The Operating Agreement

In most cases, the attorney will advise you to create a Limited Liability Company (LLC) that will take title to the property. The Operating Agreement is the legal document that governs who manages the company, how decisions are made, and how profits are distributed.

The Operating Agreement can be a simple one pager or dozens of pages long. A more complex Operating Agreement can define who can make what decisions, how these decisions are made, how people can be added or removed from the LLC, and other details.

You can download and use sample Operating Agreements from the Internet. But at the end of the day, you need to have a competent attorney create one for you or at least review the one you provide.

Your attorney may charge you $500–$1,500 for an Operating Agreement, depending on the complexity. Even though you might be the LLC's sole member, the LLC is a separate entity from you, and the Operating Agreement defines how that entity is governed. A good Operating Agreement gives you credibility with others and provides the proper legal shield if necessary. Don't skimp on this step!

The Operating Agreement defines what decisions you and your investors can make and how these decisions are made (e.g., do they require a majority vote, or do they need to be unanimous?). It may define the roles and responsibilities of each of the officers.

The agreement defines the ownership percentages of each of the members and how profits are to be distributed. It also defines other operational details, such as the end of the fiscal year and when and where the annual member meeting will be held.

Using your Operating Agreement, you can structure the LLC in several different ways. Here is a list of several options, from simple to more complex:

Scenario #1: You are the Sole Member of the LLC and have no investors. In this scenario, it's just you, and you're using your own money.

Scenario #2: You are the Sole Member of your LLC, and you are borrowing money from investors. This is like scenario #1 except that you are borrowing cash from investors who get a promissory note secured against the building (by the way, this scenario is not very common when buying apartment buildings).

Scenario #3: Your LLC has multiple Members. In this scenario, you are not borrowing money from your investors. Instead, your investors are contributing cash for a percentage of the company. You and the investors are all Members with equal voting rights. This structure may be appropriate if you're investing with a small number of friends and family partners.

Scenario #4: The LLC has Investing Members and Managing Members. Typically, the Investing Members are relatively passive, and the Managing Members make the majority of the decisions. This is the most common scenario for syndicated apartment building deals.

Scenario #5: The LLC has multiple classes of Members (i.e., Class A Investing Members and Class B Investing Members). This may be appropriate if you have one major investor who receives preferential voting rights and profit distributions over the Class B Investing Members.

Using the Operating Agreement, you can give your investors no decision-making authority at all (making them "silent" investors), or you can give them more authority. This depends on what your investors want to feel comfortable with the deal. You can also use the Operating Agreement to define how additional capital can be added at a later time, or how investors' shares can be bought out.

Don't worry too much if this sounds a bit complicated! Your attorney will ask you questions about what you want and then draft the Operating Agreement accordingly.

Security Law Considerations

What do securities laws have to do with buying apartment buildings with investor money?

When you accept funds from others to buy an apartment building, you are effectively selling shares, or securities, in the LLC that will own the building. As such, they fall under federal and state securities laws.

These laws differ by state and how complex of a deal you're putting together. Typically, you must provide your investors with a disclosure document and file some forms with your state and/or federal SEC. For example, if you have five investors who are all from the same state investing in a specific apartment building in that same state, you may have no filing or disclosure requirements.

On the other hand, if you're advertising to pool $5M from investors across the country for assets that have yet to be identified, then your disclosure and filing requirements are much more rigorous.

Most likely, your situation will fall somewhere in the middle: you're not advertising to the public to find investors; rather, your investors come to you from word of mouth and prior relationships. You will probably have less than thirty-five investors, and you're probably raising funds for a specific property you have under contract.

For a scenario like this, it's not difficult to comply, but it will cost you extra money to do so because a securities attorney will have to advise you and prepare the sixty-to-ninety-page Private Placement Memorandum (PPM). This can cost you $8,000 to $20,000 (and even more) depending on the size and complexity of the transaction.

The PPM is a rather long document with disclosures that are required to comply with securities laws.

Why would you want to issue a PPM to your investors?

The primary purpose of the PPM is to disclose all potential risks of the investment to your investors and to ultimately protect you. If you *don't* issue a PPM and the deal goes bad, your investors could contact the state or federal Securities and Exchange Commission (SEC) and file a complaint. The SEC may investigate the complaint. The first thing they'll check is if you've registered the proper disclosures. If you did, that usually ends the investigation because you've complied with securities laws. If you didn't, the SEC may prosecute and fine you. The noncompliance may also hurt you in court if the investors decide to sue you.

You have to weigh whether spending $8,000+ on a securities attorney makes sense. If you do it, you can sleep soundly at night, not having to worry about a potential SEC investigation. On the other hand, we as entrepreneurs always take well-thought calculated risks, and not issuing a PPM could be one of those calculated risks.

If your investors are generally friends and family who will not likely become belligerent, even if the deal turns bad, or if the building is smaller, you may want to forgo the extra expense and the PPM. Ask your attorney and other investors for additional data points. But you must decide for yourself what level of risk you're comfortable with.

In addition to the PPM, investors get a Subscription Agreement (SA). The purpose of the SA is for the investor to agree to the investment amount, acknowledge the receipt of the PPM, and make other disclosures required to comply with SEC regulations.

Now that we're on the same page regarding the entity and SEC-related documents required for closing, here are some tips for getting your investors ready for closing and the funds wired into escrow.

2 Simple Steps to Get Investors Funds into Escrow

Step #1: Get the investors to review and sign the documents. Investors are normally busy people and won't have a ton of time or patience to read and sign a bunch of paperwork.

Unfortunately, there are a ton of documents that should be reviewed by the investor and must be signed. I have found that some investors just sign when and where you want them to, some give you comments, and a few actually have their attorneys review the documents.

It is imperative throughout the entire process that you communicate clearly what you want done and by when, remind people constantly, and do whatever it takes to get it done.

Normally, the attorney will have the Operating Agreement ready before the PPM (since the PPM incorporates the Operating Agreement). The Operating Agreement is the most critical document for the investor to review since it is the contract between them, you, and the LLC.

Give the investors several days to review the document and submit questions and comments. Enforce your time limits by emailing reminders and, if necessary, by calling or texting the investor.

When you email the investors to review the Operating Agreement, summarize the important terms of the document. Many times, this is perfectly sufficient for the investor and they might not feel the need to review the entire document. In any event, it makes it easy for the investor to say yes and maybe saves them time.

You want to make it as easy as possible to do business with you.

The bottom line is: the investors need to sign the Operating Agreement and Subscription Agreement, but they do not need to sign the PPM.

Step #2: Ensure the funds are wired on time for closing. You're almost to the finish line! The last step is to email the wire transfer instructions to each of the investors. Give them a deadline, remind them of the deadline, and follow up if the funds aren't in the escrow account by the deadline.

As you can see, dealing with your investors can be a time-consuming process. You will find that some investors are very responsive and follow instructions while others are not so compliant. You will need to communicate frequently and patiently; be sure to allow extra time for the stragglers.

While you're off getting your investors to review and sign the documents, your SEC attorney is completing the necessary federal and state SEC forms, which he will file at closing. He will keep the signed documents in his files.

Now you're ready for closing!

CHAPTER 19

Milestone #7: Close and Cash Your Acquisition Fee Check

Here you are. You've reached one of the most exciting steps of this process—closing!

Once you received commitment for the loan and your investors have completed their paperwork and wired the funds into the escrow account, closing itself should be a "non-event" and should be over quickly.

Your closing attorney will handle all of the paperwork for closing: he or she will verify that the cash funds are in the escrow account, create the HUD-1, and manage any mortgage documents. You then go to closing (either in person or remotely with the help of a mobile notary), sign everything, you (or your property manager) grab the keys, and the building is yours!

And if you paid yourself an acquisition fee, you'll leave closing with a nice check, too!

Congratulations! You just closed your first apartment building deal!

Some of you might be asking, "That's great, Michael. I'm super excited! But what happens next?"

I don't want to keep you in a lurch with this question—because it's an important one! So before we move on to the final step of the Financial Freedom Blueprint, let's talk about what happens after closing, specifically how to manage the property to maximize cash flow and profits.

CHAPTER 20

Milestone #8: Manage the Property for Maximum Profits

You've jumped through all the necessary hoops to arrive at your final milestone!

Once you've closed on the property (and cashed your acquisition fee check!), it's now time to let your property manager take over, stabilize everything, and then implement your business plan to maximize your cash flow and profits once you refinance or sell.

In this section, I want to review ways you can add value, how to manage your property manager, and how to recognize when it might be time to part ways with your property manager.

By now you're already familiar with the power of commercial real estate. For example, if you're able to increase rents by $50 and decrease expenses by $50 per unit per month on a 24-unit apartment building, you've increased the income of the property by $28,800 per year ($100 per unit x 24 = $2,400 per month x 12 months).

Not that much, you say? It doesn't seem like much. But if you assume that the capitalization rate is 8.5% for buildings like this in this area, then your tiny increase in income increased the value of the property by $338,824.

Sound a little better?

"Yes," you say, "but how do I create this value?"

Here are eight tips to increase the income of your asset and increase the value to maximize your profits with apartment buildings:

Tip #1: Reduce your water bill. In many cases, you (the owner) are paying for your tenants' water bill. The biggest reason the building's water bill is high is because there are leaks and drips. The best way to catch these is to encourage your tenants to report them, to look for water issues whenever the property manager enters the unit, and to do regular unit inspections. Another way you can drastically reduce your water bill is to install low-flow toilets, faucets, and showerheads. There will be a capital expense to do so, but the break-even is several months, not years.

Tip #2: Reduce your heating bill. If you're paying for heat, then your heating bill will be a challenge to control. That's because your tenants will have the heat turned to full blast in the middle of winter with the windows wide open. This is why you should try to stay away from buildings where you have to pay for the heat.

A good option if you are paying for heat is a programmable thermostat. Even though the tenant could override the programming, most will not do so because it's too complicated to figure out. If set to EPA standards, programmable thermostats can save a significant amount of energy and costs.

Tip #3: Reduce your electric bill. Another way you can reduce your electric bill is to replace all lighting with energy-saving bulbs.

Tip #4: Challenge your property tax assessment. If you are buying a property substantially below its tax assessed value, you should appeal the tax assessment. The process may take several months, but it is worth it.

One of my buildings was assessed at $650,000 and had a $5,100-per-year property tax bill. I purchased it for $475,000, appealed the tax assessment, and got it reduced to $525,000, which reduced my taxes to $3,800.

Tip #5: Price shop your vendor contracts annually. Each year, price shop your insurance, trash, landscaping, janitorial, and other vendor contracts to see if you can improve over the previous year.

Tip #6: Increase rents. The most obvious way to increase income is to raise rents. This is sometimes easier said than done for a variety of reasons. However, you and your property manager should always be on the lookout for ways to increase rents.

If the rents in your building are below average in the area, ask yourself why that is. Perhaps the other apartment buildings are in better condition or offer better amenities.

Before you buy a building, be very clear what your business plan is to increase rents. You may decide that the exterior of the building needs work to look more appealing and more comparable to the competition. This may require the installation of awnings, a new sign, painted shutters, and improved landscaping. Sometimes, even minor cosmetic upgrades like this improve the curb appeal substantially and make the property more desirable.

The size of the units affects the rent. If your units are below the average size for the area, it will be tough for you to get the average market rent. If the competition has a laundry area and you don't, then this will put downward pressure on the rents as well. However, if your product at least matches that of your competition and your rents are below market, then it's time to increase rents.

If your building is in a rent-controlled area, then you can't arbitrarily increase rents as you please. Rent control laws regulate exactly how much you can increase rents. Therefore, increasing rents in a rent-controlled building can take a long time, unless you rent to Section 8/subsidized housing voucher tenants, who are exempt from rent control. The local housing authority who runs the voucher program typically pays above-market rents for their tenants, so this is a GREAT way to increase income and reduce delinquencies.

If your building is not in a rent-controlled area, then you can send a rent increase notice as soon as the lease of each tenant expires. You need to consider the impact of a rent increase on turnover expenses and vacancies, but essentially, you can ask whatever you want.

Make sure you increase the rents by something each year so that the tenants get used to an annual rent increase, even if it's very little.

Tip #7: Install laundry facilities or vending machines. Do not underestimate the income from laundry or vending machines. Let's do some quick math on a washer and dryer:

Let's assume each unit does two loads of laundry per week. Let's assume one washer load costs $1.25 and the dryer also costs $1.25. That's $5 per week or $260 per year. At a 10-cap, you just added $2,600 of value per year. If you have ten units, then you just increased the value of your building by $26,000 just by adding laundry facilities.

In addition to increasing the income, you also added an amenity to the building, which may allow you to ask a little more in rent.

Tip #8: Pass on utility expenses with the RUBS system. RUBS stands for "Ratio Utility Billing System" and may be appropriate for situations in which the constraints of space and/or construction do not allow a property to be submetered (i.e., to have separate gas, water, or electrical meters installed for each unit). RUBS can be done for almost all utilities, including water, wastewater, electric, gas, and trash.

Implementing a RUBS system often requires no upfront capital investment. RUBS uses pre-calculated formulas based on industry-wide usage statistics. Once the RUBS system is in place, each tenant receives their own utility bill, which they must pay.

While it may be technically feasible to use the RUBS system and pass your utility expenses to the tenants, you must first determine whether the market allows you to do so. If you're the only owner passing along the utility expenses to your tenants and everyone else pays for water and heat, then you may have trouble filling your units or getting market-level rent!

RUBS is most appropriate when it's customary for tenants to pay for utilities, but the building you purchased is not separately metered. If the market allows for it, RUBS is an excellent way to increase your income!

Conclusion

Making money with apartment buildings is all about creating value. What I like about apartment buildings is that even a LITTLE value can have a huge impact on PROFITS. Increasing rents a little bit here, adding laundry machines there, reevaluating your contracts and watching your utilities, all contribute a little bit to the bottom line. Multiply that little bit by the number of units for the entire year and divide it by the capitalization rate, and the result of your little improvements can mean BIG profits.

Best Practices for Managing the Property Manager

Once you've closed on the property, it's time to manage the property manager. I want to share with you some best practices I follow on a weekly, monthly, quarterly, and annual basis to make sure the building is performing to plan and maximizing my profits.

Weekly Activities

Monitor income. You need to know what's going on with your income. Which units are vacant? When will they be rent-ready? How many viewings were there? How many applications were received? Do you need to adjust the rent or offer incentives?

You also want to know which tenants are behind on their payments (also called "delinquencies"). Find out from the manager why they're behind and if legal action is necessary. I've found that the right combination is prompt legal action coupled with proactive communication.

Understand all bills paid. You want to understand exactly what bills your property manager paid last week. What was it for, and for which unit? Was it necessary? Could it have been avoided? Could it have been done cheaper?

You want a record of *every* bill the property manager paid, how much, who the vendor was, a description of the expense, and for what unit. It's not uncommon for someone else's bill to show up in your records. Errors are easily made, but only you will catch them.

Bulk trash has been a real issue in Washington, DC, for example. This is where your tenants and neighbors throw out larger items that don't fit into your trash bin. For the last year, the city has been enforcing bulk trash with hefty fines. As a result, my property manager leased a truck to go by each of their properties to pick up any bulk trash to avoid the fines. This is a great service, but each time they pick up any bulk trash, they charge me $65. In the last couple of months, I've had about three pickups per week!

Because I noticed these escalating costs in my weekly review, I was able to address the issue with the property manager. We decided to upgrade to a larger trash bin to see if that would cut down on the amount of bulk trash. We'll see if it works, but the point is that you're catching issues as soon as possible so you can make adjustments quickly.

Weekly calls with your property manager. I've found that a short weekly call with your property manager is key to staying involved with the property. Many of the key metrics you need should be available from the property manager's online management website. Review those first, and then follow up with a regular phone call to ask questions and discuss any issues.

Monthly Activities

Create the Profit and Loss report. Once per month I create the Profit and Loss statement for that month. Typically, your property manager will provide you with that report, or you can download it from the manager's online portal yourself. Your property manager will likely not track every expense (like your mortgage, real estate taxes, and insurance), and you may have to add those expenses to create the final P&L report. I like to compare the trends from month to month, as well as actuals versus projected numbers.

Review work orders. Once a month I also review the work orders. I specifically look for two things: (1) Are there any units that are costing more than others? If so, why and what can we do about it? (2) How long does it take to close out work orders? Establish an acceptable baseline with your manager and then track this metric. Work orders that don't get addressed on a timely basis can result in unwanted turnover.

Quarterly Activities

Make distributions. Once per quarter I pay myself and my investors. You already have the P&L report done from your monthly activity. The only other thing you have to do is create a cash flow and bank balance report: see what you have in the bank account and deduct any bills that are due in the next couple of months (like real estate taxes or larger repairs). Keep a reserve—this will vary, but you always want a reserve in the account! Whatever is left is money you can distribute.

Analyze turnovers. If we've turned over any units in the past quarter, I want to understand why they turned over and if there's anything we could have done differently to avoid it. I ask my property manager to talk with the tenant to find out why they're moving out. If you feel you're having an issue with turnover, one thing you can also do is to mail a questionnaire to each of the tenants with a self-addressed, stamped envelope to get feedback from them. What do they like about living at the property? What do they feel you could do better?

Yearly Activities

Review all contracts. Once per year I review all of my contracts, such as insurance, trash, landscaping, snow removal, and common-area cleaning. I may bid out some or all of these contracts to see if I can save any money.

Complete your end-of-year report. I think it's important that you write an end-of-year report—even if you don't have investors in the deal. Include the annual P&L with the monthly numbers, as well as your budgeted P&L. If the actual numbers were significantly different from your projections, explain why. What can you do differently in the next year?

Create the budget for next year. Based on the past year's performance and the changes you want to make, create the pro forma projections for the next year. Get your property manager's input and get them to commit to it. Then track your actual performance as you repeat the cycle of review and adjustment.

Conclusion

It's a mistake to let your property manager do whatever he or she wants without *any* oversight from you. Interact with your property manager at least once per week and review the key metrics regularly. If you do, you can make adjustments promptly and ensure you're on track to maximize your property's value.

Additional Resources

Please access the Companion Course for these additional resources related to managing your property for maximum profits:

- *5 Telltale Signs That It Might Be Time to Fire Your Property Manager:* These five signs are warnings that your property manager may not be all he or she is cracked up to be.

- *What Makes You More Money: Selling Now or Refinancing?* Curious to find out if holding, selling, or refinancing is the more profitable exit strategy? Then watch this video.

To access these resources, go to FinancialFreedomTheBook.com/course > Chapter 20: Manage the Property for Maximum Profits.

Now you're off to the races! You closed on the property and you're managing the manager on a consistent basis, carefully monitoring the key metrics that will maximize your profits. If the property manager is doing their job and executing on the plan, managing this property moving forward can take only an hour per week (or even less).

This is one of the main reasons I like multifamily investing: yes, the closing can be a bit stressful, but if you have a good property manager and they've stabilized the property, you can "run this business" with very little time, given the passive income and long-term wealth it can produce—more so than any other business I've seen.

Now that you've closed your first deal, something very interesting happens: The Law of the First Deal takes over, and you become a magnet for deals and money. That force is so powerful that you would need to exert extra effort to *not* do the second and third deals.

Let's explore why the Law of the First Deal is so powerful and how you can leverage it (with very little effort) to become (permanently) financially free.

CHAPTER 21

Step #7: Leverage the Law of the First Deal to Achieve Permanent Financial Freedom

The Law of the First Deal is a curious and amazing phenomenon. Nothing compares to the power it has to make you financially free if it's done with a multifamily property (of any size).

When I first introduced the Law of the First Deal, I also introduced you to several people who were able to leverage it in doing their second and third deal and become financially free.

This last step in the Financial Freedom Blueprint is the easiest because it happens nearly automatically after you do your first deal. In fact, you would have to work extra hard *not* to do the second deal. All you have to do is to receive the gift of the Law of the First Deal and just let it happen—you're now about a year or two away from replacing your income and quitting your job!

There are no further instructions needed to complete this step, so I want to explain *why* and *how* the Law of the First Deal works. Once you see how the Law works, you can actually use it to estimate your financial freedom date and income.

5 Reasons the Law of the First Deal Works

Here are five reasons the Law of the First Deal works and why the first deal is so powerful on your journey to financial freedom:

#1: You have a track record. Once you do your first deal, you now have a track record. A track record is huge, even if it's largely psychological. A track record gives you confidence, and this shines through when you speak with brokers and investors. It also qualifies you for certain loans as you do bigger and bigger deals.

#2: You have investors. To do your first deal, you likely had some investors. Once you have a handful of investors, it's much easier to get more. Also, your investors talk to their friends, and you get even more investors as word of mouth spreads. Investors beget more investors.

#3: You have a pipeline of deals. When you first got started, you didn't have a single broker feeding you deals. By the time you do your first deal, you have a network of brokers and are working a sizable pipeline. And now that brokers know you've done a deal, word spreads fast that you're a "performer." In fact, it would not be uncommon for you to have your second (larger) deal under contract by the time you close your first.

#4: You have a team on the ground, ready to go. You now have a team of professionals ready to go. You have your property manager in place. You have a good commercial mortgage broker and real estate attorney. Your team's already been through one deal together, and they're poised to do the second deal.

#5: Your confidence and comfort zone have expanded significantly. This affects everything: it expands your mind to consider larger deals, brokers don't ask you for your track record, and investors are eager to take a meeting with you. The more you educate yourself, the more you practice, and the more you push farther into deals will affect how quickly your confidence and comfort zone expands.

Joseph Gozlan: A Case Study

I shared Joseph Gozlan's story (page 36) with you earlier in the book, and it's a perfect example to illustrate this idea. In the beginning, Joseph really struggled because brokers were simply not returning his phone calls, and he wasn't getting good deal flow. By his own admission, he did not get the proper training to avoid this, but it's an example of how it can be a challenge early on.

It took Joseph two years to finally close his first multifamily deal—a 22-unit.

And then an amazing thing happened: within just six months, he closed on a 102-unit.

Why?

When he got started, he didn't have a track record, investors, brokers, or a team in place. His confidence was shaky, and his comfort zone limited. That's why it took him so long to do the first deal, and that's also why his first deal was the smallest.

It also explains why his second deal followed in rapid, almost automatic succession: by the time he closed on his 22-unit, he had a track record (which means brokers returned his phone calls), he had a pipeline of deals and investors, and his confidence was sky high.

After doing your first deal, you will become a magnet for more deals and money—it's an amazing phenomenon to behold!

Now that we know *why* the Law of the First Deal works, let's examine *how* it works. Once you understand that, you can determine how many units you need and how long it might take.

Here's how you can estimate the number of units you need to cover your living expenses and approximately how long it will take based on the Law of the First Deal.

Step #1: Determine the average Income Per Unit. The first step is to determine the average Income Per Unit, which is how much cash each unit will produce every month (on average) over the life of the investment. The way to do that is to take your financial analyzer and calculate your compensation from your share of the cash flow distributions, acquisition fees, asset management fees, and profits from a sale.

Here's an actual example from a 69-unit deal in Memphis that we closed together with a student:

	1	2	3	4	5	TOTAL
Manager Compensation						
Distributions from Cash Flow	$32,056	$34,705	$36,251	$37,828	$39,436	$180,275
Acquisition Fee	$69,000					$69,000
Asset Management Fee (1.5% of Income)	$6,900	$7,285	$7,430	$7,579	$7,731	$36,925
Capital Transaction Fee (1% of Sales Price)	$0	$0	$0	$0	$30,236	$30,236
Net Profits from Sale	$0	$0	$0	$0	$92,800	$92,800
Total Manager Compensation	**$107,956**	**$41,990**	**$43,681**	**$45,407**	**$170,202**	**$409,236**
Income Per Unit Per Month	$130	$51	$53	$55	$206	$ 99

The income is a bit "lumpy" or inconsistent because in the first year, there's a $69,000 acquisition fee, which increases the Income Per Unit in Year 1. Similarly, in Year 5, the Income Per Unit is much higher because we get a profit from the sale, as well as a 1% capital transaction fee.

The *average* Income Per Unit over the five-year period is right around $100.

This example assumes that you own 100% of the General Partnership. But maybe you brought the deal to an experienced syndicator (an excellent idea!) and you gave up 70% of the deal and your partner raised all of the money. Maybe you did a 50/50 split on your second deal, and you did the third deal all by yourself. Let's assume the average Income Per Unit for the first three deals is $75.

Step #2: Determine how many units you need. Continuing our example, let's assume your Rat Race Number is $7,500 per month in passive income. Our projected average Income Per Unit is $75, which means we would need to control about one hundred units to achieve your Rat Race Number.

Next, let's figure out how long this might take.

Step #3: Determine how long it will take. To answer this question, it's helpful to understand the progression of deal size and time line associated with the Law of the First Deal. Let's revisit how long it took some of the entrepreneurs I introduced earlier to replace their income with apartment buildings.

Drew Kniffin

- New Year's Eve 2014: Decides to pursue multifamily strategy
- + 3 Months: 3-unit
- + 1 Month: 4-unit
- + 2 Months: 32-unit

- + 6 Months: Waits to make sure income is consistent and stops working for W-2 job
- **Total Elapsed Time: 12 months**

Brad Tacia

- January 2015: Decides to pursue multifamily strategy
- + 12 Months: 12-unit
- + 5 Months: 12-unit
- + 4 Months: 63-unit, replaces income
- **Total Elapsed Time: Just under two years**

Tyler Sheff

- Day 1: Decides to pursue multifamily strategy and takes leave of absence from job
- + 6 Months: Moves into 4-plex
- + 3 Months: 10-unit
- + 3 Months: 12-unit, and replaces income
- **Total Elapsed Time: 12 months**

Joseph Gozlan

- Early 2015: Decides to pursue multifamily strategy (when he was writing $40K checks for the duplex)
- + 2 years: 22-unit
- + 6 months: 102-unit, replaces his income
- **Total Elapsed Time: 2.5 years**

From my many interviews with entrepreneurs who became financially free with apartment buildings, here is the typical time line I see with the Law of the First Deal:

- **1st deal:** 3 to 18 months from the decision to pursue multi-family investing
- **2nd deal:** Within the next 6 months
- **3rd deal:** Within the next 6 months
- **Total Elapsed Time: 1 to 3 years**

Here is the progression of deal size I observe with the Law of the First Deal:

- 2 units
- 10 units
- 30 units
- 50 units
- 100+ units

Step #4: Determine the size of your first deal. The next step is to determine your entry point into this progression (i.e., the size of the first deal). We completed this exercise during the Pre-Launch Sequence (Clarify Your First Deal (page 114)), in which we determined the size of the first deal so that it was both *meaningful* and *achievable*. In most cases, the size of the first deal depends on your goals and your personal circumstances regarding your ability to raise money.

I've found that people who need to cover $10,000 per month in living expenses tend to have some of their own financial resources and know other people with money. For them, picking a duplex as their first deal might be highly achievable but not as meaningful. On the other hand, if your Rat Race Number is $5,000 per month, getting started with a duplex might make a lot of sense.

Back to our example, if your goal is to generate $7,500 of monthly passive income to quit your job, and we determined that you need about a hundred units to do so, a good entry point might be to get started with a 10-unit building. According to the Law of the First Deal, once you decide that's what you're going to do, then you'll do that first deal sometime in the next three to eighteen months, followed by a 30- and 50-unit building in the second year. After two to three years, you'll have about a hundred units, each generating an average of $75 per month in income for you.

At that point, you are "financially free." Now you have options. You can continue working if you want to, or you could quit your job. You could stop doing deals, or you could keep on buying more properties. You now control your time to do what you want to do.

I already hear some of you saying, "Michael, the Financial Freedom Blueprint is fantastic! I can clearly see what I need to do to become financially free. But one thing, Michael. It could take eighteen months to do my first deal? That's a *really* long time. Isn't there a way to do this faster?"

CHAPTER 22
Strategies for Faster Results

We want things *now*, not in three to five years or even two to three years. Before I give you some ideas about how to accelerate the time line, let me put all of this into perspective: you're on a three-to-five-year retirement plan, right? Is that time frame too long compared to the retirement plan of most people? Is that too long when the end result is that you can quit your job and do whatever you want?

Most people say no, and they acknowledge that as far as retirement plans go, this is probably the fastest they've ever heard of. Nevertheless, twelve months seems like a long time to many people to do their first deal.

It took me a long time to do my first multifamily deal. From the time I flipped my first house to doing my first apartment deal, six years had gone by. I was distracted by shiny objects. I flipped houses, got into restaurants, traded options for a while. It took me a *long* time to figure things out, I made a lot of mistakes, and I lost a lot of money in the process.

I certainly didn't think I could do my first deal in ninety days, but many people are doing just that—and I'll show you how they've done it.

Sometimes it's a combination of focus and a bit of luck.

Take Ed Hermsen, for example. He got his first 22-unit deal just three months after signing up for my program. Taking my advice to heart, Ed recruited a property manager as one of his first team members, after interviewing nearly a dozen of them. One of them referred him to an owner who was interested in selling, and that's how he found this off-market deal. When I interviewed him on my podcast (Episode #48), just a few weeks after closing that deal, he was already working a 50-unit deal. This is the Law of the First Deal in action!

Ed did his first deal in three months. Will you get results in three months? Maybe, or maybe not. But even if it takes twelve months or longer, remember that you're on a three-to-five-year retirement plan. So what if it takes a little longer?

I know, I know. I can already hear the impatient crowd mumbling, "Yes, Michael, that's great, but do you have a shortcut up your sleeve?"

Well, I might have a few for you to consider if you want to do your first deal in ninety days.

Strategy #1: Buy a Duplex

If you want to do your first apartment building deal in the next ninety days, then consider starting with a duplex. That's exactly how Jay B., Drew Kniffin, Brooks Everline, and Tyler Sheff got started to trigger the Law of the First Deal to financial freedom.

Why is buying a duplex so much faster? Buying a duplex shortcuts the process of getting into multifamily investing for several reasons:

- **#1: There's more of them, and they're easier to find.** There are many more duplexes and quads than larger multifamily properties. You don't need to build relationships with commercial real estate brokers so that they take you seriously. Just go to realtor.com or call your local real estate agent, and you'll have dozens of duplexes to choose from.

- **#2: You need less money.** In many parts of the country, you can buy a duplex for the price of a single-family house. According to realtor.com, the median home price in the United States is $188,900. If you assume you need 20% down, you only need about $38K cash to close—a lot more doable than requiring $200,000 to buy a million-dollar apartment building.

- **#3: Duplexes are easier to analyze.** Analyzing a duplex is like buying a single-family house rental: you calculate the cash flow and potentially the post-repair value, if you're renovating, and ensure you make the cash-on-cash return you're looking for. With duplexes, you don't have all of the expenses you have with multifamily properties: you really only have property taxes, insurance, repairs, and the mortgage.

- **#4: You don't need to build a huge team.** To get into the multifamily business, you'll need to build a trusted team of property managers, attorneys, brokers, and lenders. To do your first duplex deal, you don't need to spend weeks building a team: you'll probably self-manage the duplex, and your local real estate agent will help you take care of the closing and refer you to their local lender for financing. Easy.

- **#5: Cash flow per unit tends to be better than that of larger multifamily properties.** It turns out that house rentals actually make more money per unit than larger multi's. While finding multifamily deals with a cash-on-cash return of 10% or higher might be challenging, it's considerably easier with single-family houses or duplexes.

In short, finding a duplex is easier, faster, cheaper, and more profitable per unit than a larger multifamily deal. As a result, it's not unreasonable to buy your first duplex in the first ninety days when a larger multifamily property might take longer.

Wondering how to buy your first duplex? Here's your 90-Day Checklist:

The 90-Day Checklist to Buying Your First Duplex

Here's what you're going to do in the first four weeks:

Week 1: Educate yourself. This is the same first week of the Pre-Launch Sequence: you're going to complete a course or seminar, or read all that you can about apartment building investing. While investing in duplexes is less complex than larger multifamily properties, you should still know about finding and analyzing duplexes, raising money, and managing the property.

Week 2: Determine your investing area. Decide where you're going to look. Since duplexes are more readily available, there's a good chance you can invest closer to home. For example, it's nearly impossible to find good multifamily properties in Northern Virginia where I live, but I could drive an hour and find dozens of cash flowing duplexes in smaller, rural towns.

Week 3: Analyze five deals. Here are the steps I recommend using to analyze and track your duplexes:

- Go to realtor.com and get the listings of five duplexes. Make sure you get the number of bedrooms, square footage, and rent they're currently getting from the listing broker. If they can supply you with expenses, that's even better but not required.

- Create a spreadsheet to track your deals side by side. Include the asking price, your offer price, number of units, square footage, and rental income.

- For each duplex, create a simple Profit and Loss summary. Use the rental income supplied by the listing or from the realtor and assume you'll have 10% vacancy per year. For expenses, you can use the realtor.com figures (toward the bottom of the listing) to calculate your real estate taxes, insurance, and mortgage payment. I suggest purchasing a home warranty plan ($450 per year) that has a $100 deductible. Then budget $100 per month for repairs (the larger items should be taken care of by the home warranty).

To save you some work, I created this spreadsheet for you: I call it The 10-Minute Offer Duplex Tracking Sheet, and you can download it by accessing the Companion Course.

Go to FinancialFreedomTheBook.com/course > Chapter 22: Strategies for Faster Results > Lesson #1: 90-Day Checklist to Buying Your First Duplex.

Once I have the five duplexes side by side in the spreadsheet, I evaluate each deal according to these three criteria to determine if the deal is good:

- Are the current rents at market, or is there a chance to raise them? Find out by going to rentometer.com, which will give you the median rent for similar properties in that area.

- What's the current value? What is the value of comparable properties? Are you getting a deal or overpaying? If you're renovating the property, what is the after repaired value?

- What is the cash-on-cash return? Compare the cash flow of one duplex to the cash flow of another. Does it meet your minimum return? Focus on the deals with the highest cash-on-cash return (but at least 10%).

In The 10-Minute Offer Duplex Tracking Sheet, I have a "red light/green light" section that allows you to view these side by side.

Week 4: Create your Sample Deal Package and start raising money. In this step, you create your Sample Deal Package, which looks and feels like the same document you give investors when you have a deal under contract, except that you don't actually have it under contract. To review how to create a Sample Deal Package (and to download a Word template), please go back to How to Create Your Sample Deal Package (page 50).

I realize that you may not have to raise any money if you're buying a duplex because you have the money yourself. That's one reason buying a duplex is faster—you're not spending time raising funds. But I'm incorporating it into the 90-Day Checklist to be more conservative and because it's valuable to learn the skill of raising money, whether you have your own cash or not!

To summarize: In the first four weeks, you laid the groundwork for what's next. You educated yourself, finalized your investing geography, created your deal analysis and tracking sheet, and crafted your Sample

Deal Package. For the next sixty days you're going to focus on two activities:

#1: Schedule one investor meeting per week. Using the Sample Deal Package you developed, reach out to your sphere of influence and schedule meetings with people who might be interested in investing in your first duplex deal.

If you follow this step, you'll have eight meetings, and at least one of those will agree to fund your first duplex.

If you have your own funds for the first deal—great! But I still want you to start the money raising process now, so that you have the funds for the next deal.

#2: Make five offers per week. Continue adding deals to your offer tracking spreadsheet and make offers as you go along. If you make five offers per week (not hard to do), that's forty offers in sixty days, and your goal is to get just *one* accepted (also a reasonable goal).

Bonus Downloads and Video

I assembled several bonus downloads all in one place in the Companion Course that you might find useful for this duplex strategy:

- *The 10-Minute Offer Duplex Tracking Sheet:* a spreadsheet to help you quickly analyze several duplexes side by side

- *90-Day Fast-Track Checklist to your FIRST Duplex Deal (PDF)*

- *Letter of Intent Template (Word):* Download and modify it and start making offers

- *Sample Deal Package Template (Word):* Download and modify it and use it to start raising money

- *How-To Video:* This video shows you the 90-Day Checklist to Buying Your First Duplex in action and gives you a visual of the steps I just described.

To watch the video and access the downloads, please go to the Companion Course at FinancialFreedomTheBook.com/course > Chapter 22: Strategies for Faster Results > Lesson #1: 90-Day Checklist to Buying Your First Duplex.

That's it! You've completed your ninety-day plan to buying your first duplex.

If you thought you needed tons of cash, experience, or time to get into apartment building investing, then I've got news for you:

You don't!

If you're struggling with the idea of doing a larger multifamily deal and you're about to give up, then buy a duplex. Once you have that under your belt, either do another one or shoot for something a little bigger.

Either way, you're in the game and on the path to achieving your financial goals with real estate investing!

Strategy #2: Partner to Fast-Track Your First Deal

One of the fastest ways to do your first deal is to partner with an experienced multifamily investor. Your contribution to the partnership is delivering a pre-negotiated deal on a silver platter and doing a lot of the work during due diligence and after closing. Your experienced partner can raise the money and/or leverage their track record to close the deal and get financing. Of course, this only gives you a slice of the pie, but you realize that it also gets you into your first deal. This would give you a track record, prepare you to do your next deal on your own, and trigger the Law of the First Deal.

That's how Joe Fairless, the host of the popular podcast Best Ever Real Estate Advice, did his first deal, a giant 168-unit property in Cincinnati. He partnered with an experienced syndicator to leverage his track record to get the deal under contract and help him raise the money. After doing that first deal, Joe no longer needed that partner for the second deal. To learn more, listen to Podcast #10.

Jay B., who I introduced you to earlier (page 34), also partnered with an experienced syndicator on his off-market 36-unit deal in Phoenix, Arizona. He gave up 75% of the deal and still had to raise all the money. This may be an extreme example, and perhaps I wouldn't advise giving up that much, but he doesn't see it that way. He says that, yes, he gave up a lot, but now he has his first deal, and is positioning himself for larger deals that he can do himself in the future.

It's interesting to note that many successful apartment building entrepreneurs partnered on their first deal. This is an important data point you should not ignore, and strongly consider.

At this point, you might be sold on the idea of partnering but you're unsure about how to find your potential partner.

It's easier than you think.

How to Find Your Potential Partner

Finding good deals is always a challenge, even for the experienced syndicator. For them, the problem isn't raising the money but finding enough high-quality deals. If you deliver them a deal on a silver platter, they will be eager to speak with you. I'm telling you this so you don't feel anxious about cold-calling an experienced syndicator. The truth is, if you have a deal, they *want* to hear from you.

Where do you find experienced syndicators? Here's a partial list to get you going:

- Your local REIA

- Network on real estate communities like Bigger Pockets

- Ask your team members (brokers and property managers) for referrals to owners in the area

- Contact me! I have a partnership program (www.TheMichaelBlank.com/partner) where I raise all of the money for a deal when you find and stay in the deal.

Finding potential partners is relatively easy, but approaching them in the *right* way is important if you want to get their attention.

Here's what you **don't** want to do:

I get emails like this all the time:

"I have a great deal—see attached. What do you think?"

I'm exaggerating a bit to make a point, but it's not far off. Many people think that sending a marketing package from a deal listed by a broker gets their foot in the door with an experienced syndicator.

I strongly dislike getting emails like this from people. It proves to me that they're not educated, don't respect my time, nor understand how to provide value.

Don't make that mistake. Here are some tips for approaching potential partners in a way that makes it easy for them to engage with you.

How to Get a Deal "Partner-Ready"

Before approaching a potential partner, you need to get your deal "partner-ready." That means you should ensure the deal meets the partner's general requirements, have the deal properly analyzed, and have some kind of inside track on the deal. Let's talk about each in turn.

Tip #1: Know the partner's deal criteria. Every potential partner has different investment criteria, and it's important to find out what they are—ideally, in advance. Ask them these questions:

What range of unit sizes would you consider?

What cities or areas would you consider?

Do you prefer stabilized or value-add deals?

What kind of returns (cash-on-cash and average annual return) do you need to show to your investors?

What terms do you like to see in the contract?

What would be the process for bringing you a deal?

Tip #2: Properly analyze the deal. The only way to know if the deal meets your partner's criteria is to analyze the deal with a good apartment deal analyzer so you can determine the returns. Correctly completing your financial model isn't enough. You could be 100% accurate with your model, but what research have you done and who can confirm that rents are indeed $100 under market or that the Cap Rate is 8%?

To make it easy for a potential partner to evaluate your deal, you should give them a completed financial model and be prepared to answer basic questions about your assumptions.

Tip #3: Have an inside track on the deal. In order for the deal to be truly valuable to a potential partner, you should have some kind of edge over anyone else. This might mean it's an off-market deal and you're dealing directly with the seller. Maybe you're dealing with a wholesaler who has the deal under contract, or it's a pocket-listing and the broker hasn't officially listed the deal yet and is giving you first crack at it before he markets it to his buyers' list.

Not only should you have an inside track on the deal, but you should at least have a verbal agreement on a price that makes sense. A signed Letter of Intent would be even better.

If you stick to these three tips, your potential partner will be itching to talk with you.

Now that we have a deal worth presenting, what's the best way to structure it?

How to Structure the Deal with Your Partner

As you contemplate a partnership with a more experienced partner who will raise the money for you, there are at least three types of roles and responsibilities that will determine the equity split or "General Partner Share" (the "GP Share"):

- **The "Contract Share":** 20% of the GP Share is for finding the deal and getting it under contract. This includes performing the due diligence, paying the deposit, funding the due diligence expenses, and any experience or Proof of Funds necessary to get the property under contract.

- **The "Raising Money Share":** 50% is for raising the money and securing the bank financing.

- **The "Management Share":** 30% is for managing the property after closing.

Here is an example of how this would work in practice.

Let's say you and your partner purchase a building for $2M and require $400,000 to close. The investors get 80% of the deal (this is the "Limited Partner Share" or "LP Share"), and the General Partners (you and your partner) get 20% (this is the "GP Share"). This is how you decide to split the GP Share:

- **The "Contract Share":** You find the deal, and your partner helps you analyze it and get it under contract. You split the Contract Share 50/50 so that each of you gets 10% of the GP Share (for a total of 20%, which makes up the "Contract Share" portion of the GP Share).

- **The "Raising Money Share":** You raise half the money, and your partner raises the other half. Again, you split the Raising Money Share 50/50 so that each of you gets 25% of the GP Share.

- **The "Management Share":** You're the primary manager but want ongoing support from your partner. You decide to split the Management Share 60/40, with 18% of the GP Share going to you and 12% going to your partner for his or her ongoing role in the deal.

In this example, you would get 55% of the General Partner Share, and your partner would get 45%. The terms of your arrangement would be defined in the Operating Agreement.

This is only an example, and how you end up structuring the partnership will vary, but hopefully, this methodology will allow you to negotiate a General Partnership Split with your partner that is acceptable to both of you.

How Patrick Duffy Did His First (69-Unit) Deal without Experience or His Own Money

How is it possible that a twenty-seven-year-old with no experience or capital can close his first deal, a 69-unit apartment building? I'll let Patrick tell his story:

> I was programmed like so many other people to go to college, get good grades, and get a good job. I got good grades and graduated from Harvard with a degree in finance. My family had inherited a small apartment building, and I saw from a distance that they generated mailbox money every month.
>
> After graduation, I worked for a residential lender and made loans to real estate investors, like house flippers and landlords. A few years and several similar jobs later, I decided I didn't want to continue working like this for the rest of my life. I saw these

real estate investors making money with their house flips, but I always thought it would take too long, and it was way too much work.

I then learned about apartment buildings and began looking into it. I talked to other people I met and slowly began to educate myself about apartments. I liked how passive the income was and how quickly I could replace my income.

I felt like if I could learn the lingo and find a partner, I could do this.

I joined Michael's program that allowed me to partner with him. Through that program, I was able to upload my Syndicated Deal Analyzer and get feedback from one of the coaches. That gave me the confidence to start making offers. The program also gave me "Deal Desk" privileges, which allowed me to partner with Michael if I found a good deal, and he would raise the money for it.

That's why I started to look at projects that were bigger than fifty units, even though I didn't have the money for something that big myself.

One of the guys I talked to about getting started with apartment buildings said I should consider Memphis as a location. He said property there doesn't appreciate much but the cash flow is above average for rental property. So I started looking in Memphis and came across a 69-unit on LoopNet.

I analyzed that deal, got feedback on my analysis through the program, and then made an offer. Somehow, the broker took me seriously. I was able to get a Letter of Intent signed, and then I submitted the deal to the Deal Desk.

The first step was a Deal Desk Review call, and Michael asked me questions to qualify the deal. He told me that not only had I analyzed the deal properly, but I'd researched my assumptions, and he decided to move forward with the deal. We worked out the terms for a joint venture and signed a JV agreement.

He helped me put the deal under contract, and I used a line of credit for the deposit (so that I could get more equity in the deal). Then he started working with me on the due diligence. I spoke with various property managers, I interviewed mortgage brokers, and I reviewed all of the due diligence documents we got. Finally, we met in Memphis to tour the property in person, and we decided to move forward to closing.

Michael ordered the appraisal and introduced me to the SEC attorney, who began to work on the Operating Agreement and Private Placement Memorandum. Once Michael had commitments from the investors, he asked me to get them to sign everything via DocuSign. It was just a matter of getting them to wire the funds to the closing attorney at that point. And then we met in Memphis again to close the deal!

At closing, I got my deposit back and any expenses I had before closing, plus a very nice $19,035 acquisition fee. It was awesome!

It's hard to describe how important that first deal was to me. I now feel like I could do a *huge* deal. In fact, by the time we closed this 69-unit deal, I had a 196-unit under contract! There is no question in my mind that I'll be involved with 1,000 units in the next twelve months.

Many financially free real estate entrepreneurs started by partnering with someone. That's how Patrick overcame his lack of experience and money to get into the game. The bottom-line is this: Don't let your lack of experience or capital stop you from pursuing your dreams of financial independence with apartment building investing. Instead, partner with a more experienced investor and get yourself into that elusive first deal. Once you do, the sky's the limit!

Strategy #3: Invest Passively

If you have some capital yourself, then a great way to get started with apartment buildings and do your first deal is to invest passively in someone else's deal. As an investor, you obviously enjoy the returns and the tax benefits (like any other investor). But you're investing with a bigger picture in mind because you eventually want to be the syndicator yourself.

I want to emphasize that to be a good passive investor also requires you to know the ins and outs of apartment building investing. As a passive investor, you still need to know about evaluating markets and deals, the investment process, how plausible the syndicator's business plan and exit strategy are, etc. In other words, you still need to educate yourself.

To treat a passive investment as a stepping stone to doing your own deal, find a syndicator to invest with who will help you participate more actively in the deal. Not officially perhaps, but informally. He or she might give you access to the due diligence documents, answer questions, allow you to join them on property visits, maybe even come to closing.

Investing passively in someone else's deal is a great way to do your first deal and start your journey of building passive income for yourself. Best of all, it's something you can do in ninety days or less: find an experienced syndicator who is currently raising money for a deal and invest with them.

If you like this strategy, you might *really* like the next strategy.

Strategy #4: Become a Money-Raiser

This strategy involves you partnering with other syndicators to help them raise money in return for equity as a general partner. Raising money for other people's deals is a meaningful way to build equity (and cash flow) in deals *without* having to find a deal yourself. This strategy would be a good fit for you if:

- You want to be a syndicator and you have financial commitments from investors but have not yet found a good deal.

- You *don't* want to be a syndicator; you'd rather spend time raising money and connecting investors with deals that you evaluate.

- You're a high net worth individual with access to other people with money.

This is the strategy Lane Kawaoka decided to pursue to build passive income and eventually quit his job.

Lane is a city project engineer and a licensed professional with a master's degree in civil engineering and a bachelor's in industrial engineering—both from the University of Washington in Seattle. Working as a highly paid professional in corporate America and frustrated by the traditional wealth building dogma, Lane began looking for a way out with real estate. He bought a couple of rentals but didn't like how much trouble they were and then tried some turnkey investments, which were more his style. But he couldn't figure out how to scale that to the point where he could quit his job.

That's when he started looking into multifamily investing. He liked the passive nature of his turnkey real estate investments, and he didn't like the idea of syndicating his own deals. Instead, he began conversations with other syndicators who had deals they were raising money for. Lane decided that he wanted to help these syndicators raise money, and he would receive a portion of the equity in the deal. He would become a general partner, establish a track record, and build passive income and long-term wealth. Best of all, he didn't have to find, negotiate, syndicate, and manage the deal.

Perfect for Lane!

In order to attract investors, he educated himself about apartment building investing. He then started a blog, podcast, and a meetup and became known as an expert to help passive investors make better investment decisions. He would evaluate deals on behalf of the investors and then go out and raise money for the deal.

Within several months, he had raised nearly a million dollars for various projects, ranging from private money lending deals to funding flips, rentals, and multifamily syndications. As a result, he is now a managing partner in 260+ units in Alabama, Georgia, Indiana, Oklahoma, Pennsylvania, Texas, and Washington.

If you have access to capital, or you think you might enjoy the activity of raising money, then become a money-raiser for other syndicators. Not only can you use this strategy to do your first deal in the next ninety days, it might be a fabulous way to become financially free without being the lead syndicator.

CHAPTER 23

Putting It All Together

If there's one thing I want you to remember from the book, it's this:

"The ONE THING for achieving financial freedom with real estate is to focus on your first multifamily deal."

And, class, why is that the ONE THING?

That's right, it's because of the Law of the First Deal, which says:

"The first multifamily deal (of ANY size) results in financial freedom within three to five years."

You now know the 4 Secrets of the Successful Apartment Building Investor. You've learned:

1. How to be taken seriously even if don't have any experience

2. How to analyze deals and make offers in just ten minutes (and more)

3. How to raise all the money you need for your first deal (and beyond)

4. The number one way to find the best deals

I then shared with you the 7 Steps of the Financial Freedom Blueprint:

1. Determine and reduce your Rat Race Number

2. Complete your vision map

3. Get ready with the 30-Day pre-launch sequence

4. Launch by analyzing deals, meeting with investors, and building your team

5. Build your pipeline of deals and investors

6. Close your first deal

7. Leverage the Law of the First Deal to achieve (permanent) financial freedom

And if you want results even faster, you can accelerate the Financial Freedom Blueprint with one of these strategies:

• Buy small

• Partner to fast-track your first deal

• Invest passively

• Become a money raiser

I hope by now you can see how to get started with apartment buildings today, right now, even if you don't have any prior experience or your own cash. You now know which skills to focus on and the step-by-step roadmap to follow. Whatever you do, get that first deal under wraps so you can harness the Law of the First Deal and take your first steps to becoming financially free with real estate!

It has been an honor and privilege to learn with you, and I look forward to staying connected!

EPILOGUE

The Invitation

Imagine the quarterback calling for the next play in the huddle, describing exactly where everyone should go and what they should do. His team is fired up, they break "on three!" and then … they head back to their bench.

That's kind of what the end of this book is like. You now know the exact Financial Freedom Blueprint that many have used to quit their job and live the life they always wanted. You learned about the Law of the First Deal, you saw it work for many others, and you know how and why it will work for you.

You're excited, you're ready to go, and then you put the book down, and then … nothing.

You don't take action on what you just learned.

Statistically speaking, that puts you in the 90% of people who don't apply the transformational information they learn in a boot camp or seminar. I would like to encourage you to be part of the 10% who *take action*.

An object in motion stays in motion, and an object at rest stays at rest. The best way to continue the momentum from what you just learned is to take small but continuous action. To help you with this, here is my secret to achieving any overwhelming goal: take one step at a time.

It is *so* easy to get overwhelmed. When we think about any big hairy goal we have for ourselves, we feel overwhelmed and then immediately stop pursuing it. That's why many of us who have dreams never get out of the gate—because we're paralyzed by the enormity of it all.

The solution is to do the next three best things.

No more, no less.

What are the next three things you need to do to get you one step closer to your goal? Write them down now. Then just do them. This might take you a day or a week. When you're done with your list of three things, determine the next three things you need to do, then do them, too.

Don't worry about the 101 other things that you need to do. Just concern yourself with the next three.

Let's say you do this for three months. Then you look up to see what you've accomplished, and you are absolutely amazed at how far you've come.

Why Does This Technique Work So Well?

It works because the next three things bring you closer to your goal without overwhelming you. I bet if I asked you for the next three things you should do to get started with apartment building investing, you'd be able to tell me. Then just do those three things.

Let's say your goal is to do your first apartment building deal (about ten units) but you don't have any prior experience; you have about $10,000 of your own money and no investors.

Should you not even bother? Or should you do the next three things?

What are the next three things you should do?

What does the Financial Freedom Blueprint say?

Educate yourself. Continue your education to learn all aspects of buying apartments and raising money. Go on Amazon and Google and search for apartment building investing resources. Make sure you access the free Companion Course to this book (FinancialFreedomTheBook.com/course). If you're a bit more serious, you'll probably want to invest in a training program to master the 4 Secrets of the Successful Apartment Building Investor. You're welcome to consider mine, but there are others. It doesn't matter, as long as you educate yourself.

Three weeks go by, and you read two books and completed the online program. What's next?

What does the Financial Freedom Blueprint say?

Reduce your living expenses and complete your Vision Map and 90-Day Plan. It takes you a week to put the plan in place for both. Now what?

What does the Financial Freedom Blueprint say is next?

The Pre-Launch Sequence is next. Over the next thirty days, you'll become really clear about your first deal, you'll analyze five deals and complete your Sample Deal Package. You now have the minimum knowledge, skills, and confidence to be released into the world without sounding like a newbie! Look how far you've come in the last two months!

Each week you analyze deals and make offers. You reach out to the people you know and share your enthusiasm, and you schedule one meeting with a potential investor per week. You speak to one potential new team member (property manager or lender) each week.

You still have your full-time job, so you can only do this in your spare time. But after three months you've completed a course, read two books, analyzed twenty deals, and met with four investors, one of which seemed very interested in investing with you.

WOW! Isn't that amazing?

Do you still have a long way to go to find and close your first deal? Sure, but don't think about that; it'll just overwhelm you. Just focus on the three next best things and do them. If you do this, you'll be amazed at what you've accomplished. Your first deal will happen; it's now just a matter of time.

Do you see the pattern? The power of this book's approach is in the Financial Freedom Blueprint. If you trust yourself to this plan, it will lead you step-by-step toward your goal. You just have to take action, trust yourself to the process, and don't let the task overwhelm you.

I hope you found this book to be a good investment of your time. It took me over a decade to figure out the Financial Freedom Blueprint, and I shared with you only those things that have worked for me and other entrepreneurs.

Additional Resources

Regardless of how good this book might be, it can never be as good as personally working with me or one of my coaches to help you do your first deal. Therefore, I invite you to consider our coaching program, which closely follows the steps in the proven Financial Freedom Blueprint and is designed to get you into your first deal in twelve months. The program includes everything you need to be successful, including the Syndicated Deal Analyzer, the Ultimate Guide to Buying Apartment Buildings with Private Money Online course, the Deal Maker's Mastermind (for community, support, and Deal Desk privileges), and group or one-on-one coaching. Not everyone needs or can afford coaching, and I believe you will eventually achieve your goals without it. But I have observed that coaching will help you achieve your goals much faster and help you avoid costly mistakes along the way. To find out more about our coaching program, please visit www.TheMichaelBlank.com/coaching.

Regardless of whether you join our program or not, make sure you get the support you need to be successful.

If you'd like to experience what it's like to do your first deal, then I'm really excited to tell you about the Financial Freedom Summit held throughout the year. This is an advanced workshop in which participants work in small groups to do their first deal from start to finish. You will find, analyze, and negotiate a deal. You'll then do due diligence, raise money, and secure financing. Your team will need to deal with some twists and turns like in a real deal, and hopefully you'll close the deal and cash a nice acquisition fee check. This is designed to be just like a real deal but all in the course of a weekend. Participants have found that the Financial Freedom Summit expanded their comfort zone and gave them the confidence to do their first deal themselves.

A Final Word

In 2013 a nurse by the name of Bronnie Ware published a book called *The Top Five Regrets of the Dying*. As a palliative care nurse, she spent time getting to know people in the last days of their lives. Having nothing left to lose, these people shared with her their honest thoughts about life and death and what they would have done differently if they had a chance.

You know what the top two regrets were?

The #1 regret was that they had not pursued their dreams but, rather, lived a life that others wanted them to live.

You know what #2 was?

The #2 regret was wishing they hadn't worked so hard.

Wow.

Isn't that what we've been talking about? Not working so hard so that we can pursue our dreams, the life we were meant to live (a more abundant life)?

Here's my challenge to you: You're working hard right now anyway. Why not work hard for the next few years building your portfolio so you don't have to work hard later?

Decide right now to put a plan in place that will provide financial freedom for you and your family.

Decide to get started with apartment buildings right now. I've given you the Financial Freedom Blueprint, and I've shown you how to do it, even if you don't have any prior experience or your own cash.

Remember that "it is in your moments of decision that your destiny is shaped."

Once you truly decide to change your life with apartments, you *will* be financially free in three to five years.

Decide. Right. Now.

And when you do, your life—and the world—will never be the same.

I'm so grateful you've allowed me to share this space with you. I thank you for taking the time to learn with me. I wish you freedom, peace, and joy.

Michael Blank

A Quick Favor, Please?

Before you go, can I ask you for a quick favor?

Good, I knew I could count on you.

Would you please leave a review for this book on Amazon?

Reviews are very important for authors, as they help us sell more books and enable us to keep writing.

Please take a quick minute to go to Amazon and leave this book an honest review. I promise it doesn't take very long, and it will play a huge part in the success of this book and helping others become financially free.

Here is the redirect link to the book on Amazon:

www.TheMichaelBlank.com/freedom-book-amazon

Thank you again for reading,

Michael

About the Author

Michael Blank is the leading authority on apartment building investing in the United States. He's passionate about helping others become financially free in 3-5 years by investing in apartment building deals with a special focus on raising money. Through his investment company, he controls over $24 million in performing multifamily assets all over the United States and has raised over $6M. In addition to his own investing activities, he's helped students purchase over 1600 units valued at over $55M through his unique "Deal Desk" and training programs. He's the author of the best-selling book "Financial Freedom With Real Estate Investing" and the host of the popular "Apartment Building Investing" podcast. To learn more about Michael, please visit www.TheMichaelBlank.com.